Margaret Mahy

24 HOURS

Aladdin Paperbacks
New York London Toronto Sydney Singapore

This book is a work of fiction. Any references to historical events, real people, or real locales are used fictitiously. Other names, characters, places, and incidents are the product of the author's imagination and any resemblance to actual events or locales or persons, living or dead, is entirely coincidental.

First Aladdin Paperbacks edition October 2001
Copyright © 2000 by Margaret Mahy

Aladdin Paperbacks
An imprint of Simon & Schuster Children's Publishing Division
1230 Avenue of the Americas
New York, NY 10020

Also available in a Margaret K. McElderry Books hardcover edition.

Designed by Angela Carlino.
The text of this book was set in Baskerville BE Regular.
Printed and bound in the United States of America.
2 4 6 8 10 9 7 5 3 1

The Library of Congress has cataloged the hardcover edition as follows:
Mahy, Margaret.
24 hours / Margaret Mahy.—1st ed.
p. cm.
"A Vanessa Hamilton book"—T. p. verso.
Summary: During his first twenty-four hours after finishing high school, seventeen-year-old Ellis unexpectedly becomes part of an inner-city world far different from his comfortable life, which helps him deal with his best friend's recent suicide.
ISBN 0-689-83884-0 (hc.)
[Suicide—Fiction. 2. New Zealand—Fiction.] I. Title.
PZ7.M2773 Tw 2000 [Fic]—dc21 99-058947
ISBN 0-689-83903-0 (Aladdin pbk.)

To Craig–

*In celebration of the
number-one haircut*

M. M.

PART 1

5:10 P.M.—FRIDAY

Home. Home from school. Holidays. And here he was—out on the town, but on his own. As he walked through the early evening, bright with midsummer light, Ellis saw the city center glowing like a far-off stage. But, although the sunlight was finding its way so confidently between hotels and banks, shops and offices, the city was threatened by a storm. To the north, between glassy office buildings, he could see bruised clouds, polished by a lurid light, rolling across the plain toward the town.

Most of the other people in the street were going in the same direction as Ellis, probably making for the cinema complex that dominated the eastern end of the city center. He looked with interest at the few faces coming toward him, half hoping to see someone he recognized. However, as yet, he had not seen a single person he knew.

3

I can always go to a film, he thought, and patted his back pocket as if the money there were a good-luck charm.

The traffic lights changed. Glancing to the left as he crossed the street, Ellis saw the city council had installed new streetlights since he had last walked that way. Retreating, like precisely spaced blooms in a park garden, they rose on long green stems that curved elegantly at the top, then blossomed into hoods of deep crimson. FOLEY STREET, announced brass letters on a black background. At the far end of the street he saw the old library he had visited regularly as a child, bracing its stone shoulders against a constricting cage of platforms, steps, and orange-colored piping. Wide dormer windows looked toward Ellis from under deep, dipping lids, tiled with gray slate. Several streets away, a new library, complete with a computerized circulation system and a much-praised information retrieval program, would no doubt be working busily. But the old building was still there, transformed into apartments, one of them owned, he suddenly remembered, by country-dwelling friends of his parents. He guessed, looking at the scaffolding, that the company that had bought the old library must be adding a third floor to the original two. More changes, thought Ellis a little ruefully, although he also wanted the city to surprise him in some way—to put out branches . . . break into leaf . . . burst into gigantic laughter.

Free, thought Ellis, and he might have skipped a little if it had not been such a childish thing to do. Well, not quite free. University next year—okay! Okay! That was decided. But, after all, the university had a drama society and a proper theater, so they must need actors. And he would have adventures, moments of revelation, sex, even love. The coming year, he decided, would be a year of transformation. *I'm going to be an actor,* said the voice in the back of his head. *I really am!*

I am going to be an actor, Simon had also declared last year, casually but quite definitely. And then, later . . . forget acting! "I'm into sex these days," he had said when Ellis, excited by the prospect of the Shakespeare Fantasia planned for the end of the year, had auditioned successfully for the part of Claudio in a scene from Shakespeare's *Measure for Measure.* But, only two weeks after saying this, Simon had killed himself. He had, after all, been into something much more dangerous than sex. He had been in love, and love had failed him.

Somewhere behind Ellis on Foley Street a clock struck the quarter hour with a soft but significant chime. *"Now!"* that final fading stroke seemed to declaim. "It begins *now!*" And, as it faded, almost as if its echo had triggered an event in the outside world, Ellis caught sight of himself in a mirror, framed by blue tiles, linking two shops. He saw, before he strode past, the long oval of his face smiling out of a halo of curls. Not bad! he thought, glad that the quickly moving reflection had seemed to belong to someone so much older than seventeen. Yet, almost at once he felt discontented, for he did not want to look quite so wholesome—quite so new.

But now, out of nowhere it seemed, a huge wind came funneling down the street toward him. Abruptly, the air whirled with leaves and trash, some of which danced higher and higher, lifting over the streetlights, zigzagging, twisting, before tumbling away across roofs on the opposite side of the road. One piece of screwed-up red paper spun upward as if it were about to go into orbit. A blackboard, advertising café meals, tumbled toward him like a square wheel, first one corner and then another striking the pavement. Ellis dodged it. The wind punched his face, at the same time stinging him with gritty dust. Angry voices filled his ears, and a gliding figure, apparently lifted by the storm, leaped from the pavement onto a narrow, empty strip designated as a bus stop. The skater swung so dangerously close to the line of slow-moving traffic that one or two drivers tooted their horn in outrage, and a passenger lowered his window to shout angrily, "What do you think you're playing at, you bloody fool?" But the gliding man simply flung out his left arm, in a gesture both graceful and confident, and extended a single, insulting finger. Another gust of wind tilted advancing pedestrians back on their heels, and the skater, perhaps taking advantage of their uncertainty, jumped from the bus-stop space to the pavement. Suddenly, Ellis and the skater were face-to-face.

For the first time that evening Ellis recognized

someone, and was sure that he, too, was recognized. The skater's expression changed. Sliding past Ellis, he turned into a shop doorway, spun around, and then darted back again. He seemed to move without any effort at all . . . a young man in an ancient camel-hair coat, both elbows worn through, one of them blackened as if the wearer had casually leaned among red-hot coals. A name came into Ellis's head. Jackie, wasn't it? Jackie Kettle? No! Not quite! A voice from the past spoke softly in his memory. "Funny name, isn't it? It's a strange cow." Jackie *Cattle*! That was it. Jackie Cattle.

5:20 P.M.—FRIDAY

"**Yay!**" Jackie was shouting, circling Ellis. "How's it going?"

"Jackie!" said Ellis, proud of remembering the name and anxious to reassure its owner. "Oh, well! Okay! You know!" He waggled his fingers, vaguely suggesting that things were just what anyone might expect them to be . . . a bit of this, a bit of that, good and bad mixed.

Raised unnaturally high on his Rollerblades, Jackie was staring down at Ellis with friendly interest, but Ellis could easily see that something indefinable was going on behind those beaming blue eyes . . . some sort of guess was being made. He knew he was being assessed. And now he remembered that, years ago, Jackie Cattle, a confused victim for the most part, had also had moments when he could seem quite sinister.

So he gave a hasty smile—a nod, a shrug—half offering to move on. But Jackie smiled back at him—a smile bright with unconvincing innocence, revealing a clownish gap between his two front teeth. He grabbed Ellis's arm.

"Long time no see, mate!" he shouted, the wind snatching at his words.

"I've been away," Ellis shouted back.

"What? Inside?" Jackie asked with a sort of confused incredulity. "Jail?" Then he flung up his hands in a gesture of apology. "No! Of course not! Not you! Sorry!" All the time his eyes were flitting over Ellis with the attentive curiosity of someone planning to paint a portrait from memory. "So! Where the hell have you been?"

Automatically, Ellis was piecing together a memory portrait of his own. Before he had been sent to Saint Conan's school he had attended a small state one across the road from his home. Jackie Cattle had also been a pupil there, a boy at once exotic and pathetic, a year ahead of Ellis and old in his class. He must be nineteen by now, thought Ellis. Twenty, perhaps. In some ways he hadn't changed much. He still had the same round, childish face, the same heavy-lidded eyes, the same sly, sideways smile.

"I've been at school!" Ellis yelled into the storm without thinking.

"*School!*" exclaimed Jackie, bending forward as if he could hardly believe what he was hearing. He sounded much more astonished at the thought of school than he had been at the possibility of jail.

"I'm out now," said Ellis. "What about you?"

"Cross my heart, you wouldn't want to know," said Jackie, making a face.

He certainly looked disreputable–had always looked disreputable–and yet, for all that, he spoke with an accent that was almost elegant. His family had been well-to-do, hadn't they? Adults had exclaimed over the contrast between Jackie and a clever, older sister. Anyhow, the contrast between the tattered camel-hair coat and the smooth way of speaking made Jackie hard to place. Ellis found he was not quite sure how to talk to him.

"Oh, well, see you around!" he said, knowing already that Jackie was not going to let him walk away. And sure enough, Jackie's grip on his arm tightened a little.

"No! No, wait!" he cried, while his eyes ran over Ellis yet again with that same persistent speculation. "What are you rushing off for? You're not meeting a girl or anything, are you?"

"No," said Ellis a little aggressively, because Jackie had sounded so completely certain that Ellis would not be meeting a girl.

Jackie beamed. "Well, that's okay, then! Let's mingle! Be part of café society. I'll buy you a beer."

Why not? thought Ellis. I might as well find out what's going on. "Why not!" he said aloud. "I'll pay," he added, remembering he had money in his back pocket.

"Even better!" said Jackie fervently. He twitched his battered coat into place as carefully as if it had been freshly cleaned and pressed and there were some purpose in looking after it. Then he pointed backward over his shoulder with his thumb. "Follow me," he said, spinning on the spot as he extended his arm, pointing dramatically. They moved off together, Jackie gliding at Ellis's right shoulder like an escorting angel.

"So! School!" he reminisced. *"School!"* he repeated as if he were mentioning something so peculiar he couldn't quite believe in it anymore. "And what now? Got a job lined up?"

"I'm going to be an actor," said Ellis, feeling he could safely practice this announcement on someone like Jackie. It came out well—crisp, assured, and unapologetic.

"Crash hot!" said Jackie, though Ellis suspected he would have said the same thing if he, Ellis, had announced that he was planning to be an accountant.

"I only got home last night. I'm just getting used to things again," Ellis added quickly.

"Hey, you never get *used* to things," Jackie said. "Take it from one who knows!" He had one of those faces that flared into life when he smiled. The little gap between his front teeth flashed—a flash of darkness. Ellis tried to imagine a gap-toothed Hamlet. Why not? There weren't any orthodontists in Shakespeare's day.

For all that, he found he couldn't quite imagine Hamlet with a gap in his front teeth. "Why did your parents send you away to school?" Jackie asked. "Were they trying to get rid of you, or what?"

"It was my dad's old school," said Ellis. "He loved it there, and he thought I would, too."

"I'd have hated it," declared Jackie with complete certainty.

"It was all right," said Ellis.

The wind flung fistfuls of rain in their faces, drops flying toward them like transparent bullets.

"Okay! Swing right!" Jackie commanded. "In here."

A couple of minutes later Ellis was sitting at a table in a café bay window, with an oblique view of the city center. Because it was so well lit, and yet a little distant, he was teased again by the idea that he was looking onto a stage, and that someone was busily operating a wind machine in the wings.

Jackie slid back from the bar, where he had been talking in a familiar way with a barman. He was carrying two short, brown bottles of beer, a glass upended on top of one of them, and a bowl of mixed nuts and potato chips, which he passed to Ellis. Then he slumped into his chair and put the bottle to his mouth, sensuously kissing its brown lips. Ellis put the glass to one side and drank from the bottle, too.

"Saves the washing up," he said.

Jackie grinned, his grin hyphenated by darkness. "So, let's just watch the world go by for a minute or

two," he said. "Then, if you like," he added with a sly-
ness that was not intended to deceive, "we can take off
for a party I know about. Well, we can if you've got
wheels. Bigger wheels than mine, that is," he added,
glancing down at his Rollerblades.

"Oh, I see," Ellis replied with satisfying irony.
"You're not just—you know—being nice!"

"No way, mate!" exclaimed Jackie indignantly.
"This is straight-out exploitation. Trust me!"

"Suppose I don't have a car?" Ellis asked. "What'll
you do? Skate to the party with me running beside
you?"

"But you *have* got a car," said Jackie. "I took one
look at you and I just *knew*! 'Now, there's a man with a
car,' I said to myself, and I was right, wasn't I?"

He spoke drowsily, almost absentmindedly. But
there was something far from sleepy moving in the
eyes behind those heavy lids.

"It's my mother's car," said Ellis. "I'm supposed to
be home in"—he looked at his watch—"in about an
hour."

"Did you promise?" asked Jackie.

"Well, I didn't exactly promise . . . ," said Ellis.

Jackie relaxed. "Thank God," he said. "You really
frightened me then, because you're probably one of
those pricks who keep their promises. It would have
ruined everything."

"What I *am* is the prick with the car," Ellis reminded him.

Jackie laughed and nodded. "Yeah! Right! Nice

one!" he said. "Now—this party! It's out along the highway . . . a country party. I *could* skate, but it would be easier if you drove me."

Ellis remembered he had promised himself wild adventures and no apologies. And, after all, he had made his mother no real promises. "Okay, then!" he said.

Immediately, a new ease engulfed Jackie, who flopped back in his chair.

"Your turn to tell me," Ellis went on. "What have *you* been up to?"

"Oh, about up to here," said Jackie, leaning sideways in his chair and holding his hand, fingers splayed, about an inch from the ground. "No real job. No self-respect. Mind you, the way I see it, self-respect is the easiest sort of respect to get, isn't it? Me—I want respect with a bit more challenge to it." He eased himself upward in his chair once more as he went on talking. "I make a few dollars here and there, but basically I just fiddle around. I'm a born fiddler."

"Yeah, I can tell," said Ellis.

A piece of wastepaper whirled past the window and disappeared into the deepening summer evening. The city was still embraced by a largely tearless storm. Jackie slapped his hand down hard on the table. "Five! Four! Three! Two! ONE!" he exclaimed, leaping to his feet and draining the rest of his beer. The movement upward married into a movement forward. "Blastoff!" he cried.

Before Ellis's eyes he became charged with both energy and mischief. Hastily, Ellis drank half his beer, and then, remembering he would be the driver, left the rest of it on the table. He followed Jackie into the street, and they wove their way, side by side, back to the parking lot where Ellis had left his mother's car.

"Straight down the Great North Road," said Jackie, scrambling into the passenger seat. "It's a sort of barbecue party. Begins—officially, that is—with five o'clock drinks. So, by the time we get there, they mightn't care who's turning up. Unless they've been rained out."

"If it's an inside party, they mightn't let us in," said Ellis almost hopefully. He wanted the adventure, but felt dubious about crashing a private party.

"Why not?" said Jackie, sounding affronted. "I mean, look at us: clean, smiling! Both respectable guys! Yes?"

Ellis felt certain that Jackie had chosen him not merely because he had a car, but because his curling hair and tidy clothes might persuade someone, somewhere to welcome them in.

5:50 P.M. – FRIDAY

They surged onto the highway, heading north, and the suburbs fell away altogether. As they moved deeper into the country, Ellis felt a change coming over Jackie Cattle. He had not understood just how tense his companion had been until Jackie shifted in the seat beside him, sighing as he relaxed.

They crossed a long bridge curving over one of the five rivers that braided and divided the plains between city and mountains, and Ellis glimpsed, below him, threads of water winding, separating, then weaving together again, negotiating wide, flat beds of gray shingle. Gusts of wind beat the river surfaces into angry, gray green ripples ticked with silver.

"Next turnoff, move into the left lane," Jackie instructed, smiling in secret satisfaction.

Oh, no! Ellis thought automatically. He had been driven along this highway, turning left at that very

16

corner, many times throughout his childhood, and never with any pleasure. Come off it! he told himself derisively as they curved away from the highway and onto a long, straight road with fences, hedges, and occasional gateways on either side. Just because . . ., he began thinking, then forced himself to notice the roadsides as if he had never seen them before. Some gates had signs beside them listing fruit and vegetables that could be bought during the day, but most signs were lying flat on the grass, flapping and bucking wildly as the wind pushed powerful fingers under them. One particular sign, hanging by short chains from a wooden support that reminded Ellis of a gallows, was stretched out almost parallel to the ground, straining to escape. The words FRESH LETTUCE, TOMATOES, AVOCADOS angled into sight, then vanished once more.

But they were driving out of the path of the storm. The road ahead was suddenly dry. Hedges and trees that had been writhing on either side of the road were suddenly less convulsive, the sideways thrust on the car much less insistent.

It was hard for Ellis to imagine any connection between the friends of his parents who lived along this road and disreputable Jackie Cattle, and yet he felt himself touched by apprehension. Don't be crazy, he kept telling himself. There are a dozen places out this way. We'll probably drive on past, and . . .

"Big white gates!" announced Jackie, leaning forward.

Oh, no! Ellis sighed to himself in fatalistic despair. The familiar gates were rushing toward him on his right–big old gates, white, pointed palings like teeth between high stone posts, also painted white.

"White gates," repeated Jackie. "And chestnut trees! This must be the place!"

Ellis was already turning in at the gates, noting festive balloons tied to the rural delivery mailbox. Though the wind was gentler now, the balloons still strained and bobbed furiously like a huddle of demented heads. But the car glided confidently past them and on between the double line of chestnut trees. Even though he was sitting correctly in the driver's seat, his hands on the wheel in a two o'clock position, Ellis felt his mother's car, which had turned in at that gate many times before, was really finding its own way. Every cell in his body seemed intent on turning and going back to town again. But there, in front of him, set in orchards and wide lawns, sprawled the house, casually impressive among its old trees.

"Oh, wow!" breathed Jackie.

Suddenly the air grew rich with the smell of barbecued steak and fish. Salmon, no doubt, wrapped in foil, cooking in its own juices, thought Ellis, remembering other barbecues in this very place.

Beside him, Jackie pulled his knees up, bending and writhing inside his coat as he struggled to remove his Rollerblades. Ellis parked at the end of a long row of cars, then turned toward him. "We'd better walk the last bit," he said, looking dubiously at Jackie's socks, which were full of holes.

"I'll go barefoot," said Jackie, peeling off his socks. "I'll look really laid-back!"

"What about your coat?" asked Ellis, knowing just what sort of party they were going to walk into. "It's a warm evening."

"Take off my coat?" cried Jackie. "Are you mad? My life story's written on this coat. See this stain here? That's a quarrel with my father, and this smear—"

"Okay! Okay!" Ellis sighed, waving his hand, palm outward, at Jackie. "I just thought you'd be more comfortable if—"

"You think I'd sacrifice truth for comfort?" cried Jackie, settling the coat across his shoulders with a complacent grin. "It will be *good* for everyone here to see a coat like mine."

Directly in front of them, between two silver birches whose upper branches had grown together to form an arch, Ellis saw the familiar triple garage, set beyond a turning space. He saw a shiny red car parked at such a careless angle that it blocked the main garage door, just as if the owner knew no other car would need to come or go, or did not much care, anyway. Ellis grimaced in spite of himself as he and Jackie strolled toward the bricked side of the house, Jackie stepping carefully on fallen leaves and grass clippings spread across fine, sharp gravel. Earlier in the day someone had mowed these verges. Ellis slunk along guiltily, but Jackie, who had absolutely no right to be there (Ellis was sure), stepped out as confidently as if his bare feet were perfectly acceptable. The wind seemed anxious to push them away, but as they came round the corner of the house, the sound of many voices swelled toward them.

"Don't look so *furtive!*" muttered Jackie. "Chill out, man!" He improvised a dance step. "Just stroll on in and say, *'Hey, folks! Your lucky day! Here we are! Now the fun begins!'*"

"I don't look furtive," said Ellis indignantly. "And I know this crowd, which I reckon you *don't*. The Kilmers are friends of ours—friends of my parents, that is! They've got one of those apartments in the old library, but this is their *real* home. I've visited them twenty million times before." He looked sideways at Jackie, half expecting to see capitulation of some kind, or even respect (because, after all, the Kilmers were rich). But in the clear, early twilight, Jackie's expression was that of a child seeing a vision of wonder. Then he flung an arm across Ellis's shoulder.

"Hey, Ellis!" he cried softly. "Has anyone told you how beautiful you are? A car! Naturally curly hair! And rich friends! The lot! I love you! I love you! And, hey, isn't that sunshine? Let's enjoy ourselves."

6:30 P.M.—FRIDAY

Ellis stepped onto the wide, grassy terrace that led down from the veranda of the Kilmers' house to the garden below, a familiar enchantment immediately taking hold of him. For there it all was: women in summer dresses, laughing and talking, leaning sexily into the intrusive wind; men in shorts hoisting long glasses of pale gold lager. Elegant music came toward them in gusts and then retreated. Ellis recognized it as the theme tune of a television commercial in which an expensive car moved with grace and power through a bare, sculptural landscape. Farmers on horses (along with their dogs) watched the car go by with admiration and envy, and a beautiful woman studied it with voluptuous attention.

Jackie seemed to react to the gusts of music, too. He came to a standstill, and Ellis saw him grimace.

"Vivaldi!" he exclaimed, half turning toward Ellis. "Poor bugger! Mind you, those musical jokers wrote a

220124

lot of stuff for parties, didn't they?" Ellis found he had assumed, yet again, that, in spite of his unexpected accent, Jackie was a man without culture. "I mean, it's so beautiful," Jackie added. "But, by now, whenever I hear it going, *Tah dah dah dah da-da dah,* I want to laugh at it. It's become its own sort of joke. And it wasn't meant to be *funny,* was it?"

"Ellis!" called an astonished voice.

"Who is it?" hissed Jackie.

"Meg Kilmer! Hostess. Lives here," Ellis muttered, grinning studiously at his mother's friend, Meg, and feeling suddenly treacherous. Why–*why*–had Jackie been so desperate to come here? There must have been other parties he could have crashed–parties that were much more his sort of thing. He, Ellis, might have unwittingly helped an enemy insinuate himself. For he was with Jackie, whose coat had one elbow burned out of it, who was barefoot, who was laughing at the idea of Vivaldi being played as background music, but who was, also, at that very moment, turning to greet the hostess with a wide smile.

"Ellis . . . lovely to see you," Meg cried, seeming only slightly surprised that he should be there at all.

"Just passing!" Ellis said, smiling, too–the sort of frank, boyish smile a friend of one's mother could trust–an actor's smile. "Didn't know you were having a party. Sorry!" He was relieved to find just how easily deception came to him. Though, after all, he hadn't known: he was speaking the truth.

"Well, we did invite Kit and Dave," said Meg

Kilmer, referring to Ellis's parents, "but Kit said she was having a few friends round tonight. Of course, she may have felt shy. People think it's a bit strange celebrating a separation."

"Well, I think the Robsons are coming over," said Ellis, his voice hesitant, wondering if he had really heard Meg say what she appeared to have said. His voice seemed to come and go in his own ears. "But Jackie and I–oh, this is my friend, Jackie Cattle, by the way. And Jackie, this is Meg Kilmer, who lives here– well, we've been cruising around–"

"Ellis shot home from school last night," interrupted Jackie, speaking rather more easily than Ellis himself. "He's getting himself reacquainted with this part of the world."

Ellis saw Meg exchange a worldly glance with Jackie at the expense of a younger man.

"Well, lovely to see you," said Meg warmly. "Go down to the lower lawn by the barbecue. There's masses to eat and drink." In spite of his ease and open smile, she was suddenly studying Jackie rather more intently. Ellis saw her expression change slightly–as if something was disturbing her. He felt she was aware of something rather more anarchic than either Jackie's bare feet or battered coat. And Jackie, too, seemed to recognize her doubt.

"I don't want to push in," he said, smiling with old-world courtesy.

"Oh, you're welcome," Meg said, relaxing a little. "We always overdo things, so there's plenty." Someone called her name. She turned, laughed, and retreated, then looked over her shoulder, pointing vaguely into the crowd.

"Christo's somewhere around," she called. "Be nice to him! He's so *grumpy* these days."

Jackie and Ellis moved across the upper lawn between groups of chattering guests, nearly all protecting piled cardboard plates and glasses of wine from the wind, then down three wide, stone steps to a lower lawn. In spite of the big, brick barbecue, it was much less crowded, perhaps because the shade of tall lime trees imparted an early twilight to this part of the garden.

"So you don't want to push in," muttered Ellis as they walked toward two long tables covered with bottles and plates. "You know, you're a real bull artist!"

"It's my gift," Jackie replied, "and we ought to use our talents. The Bible says so."

"You do what the Bible says?" Ellis asked, leaning back from Jackie and studying him with exaggerated skepticism.

"When it's in my interests," Jackie replied, his own smile vanishing.

Alan Kilmer came to meet them with a bottle of wine and what was left of a jug of beer balanced on a tray. He was wearing a striped apron and a cook's hat with the word CHEF printed on it in flowing letters.

"I suppose you drink all the beer you can get these days, young Ellis," he cried in the voice of a surrogate father keen to show how understanding he could be.

"I'm driving . . . ," Ellis said, and had a vision of the

curls and the clean, open face that had flickered briefly across the mirror panel in the city street.

"Oh, one won't hurt you," Alan said, "though you're right to be careful. I only wish Christo was careful. . . . But you're a big boy now. Take it! Food and plates over there by the barbecue. I imagine you've heard our news? Meg and I are separating. After all, Sophie's left home—she's over in Sydney doing *very* well, and of course Christo's grown up."

"Gosh, I didn't know . . . ," began Ellis.

"It's *time*," said Alan, a touch of mysticism creeping into his voice. "Meg and I both feel these rites of passage deserve celebration." His voice became friendly and fatherly again. "Now, just help yourselves."

"We haven't come to *eat*–," Ellis began guiltily.

"We're starving," declared Jackie, interrupting before Ellis could reject the offers of food and drink, or ask for Kilmer family news.

"Well, cram in all you can," said Alan cheerfully. "We always cater for too many people. The steak's from our own beast . . . but it'll be dog food by tomorrow. Strike while the sausage is hot, eh?"

Together, Jackie and Ellis made their way to the table by the barbecue. Plates of steak and sausages sat beside huge, wooden bowls of salad, the meat drying a little, the lettuce leaves starting to wilt around the edges. Jackie piled a plate with salad and sliced tomatoes, as well as a filet of salmon, glittering in a wrap of tinfoil.

"Have some steak," said Ellis. It seemed the least

25

they could do was eat the food most likely to be left over.

"I'm vegetarian—all but," said Jackie.

"You?" cried Ellis incredulously.

"I said, 'All but!'" Jackie replied, snapping a piece of garlic bread from its loaf. "I'm not above stocking up when it's free, *and* probably going to be thrown out, anyway. That's another of my virtues . . . I don't waste anything. Let's move before the Killers close in again and begin telling you about the civilized way they're managing their separation."

"Kilmers!" Ellis corrected him, not quite wanting to expose old friends to alien derision, and slightly irritated because Jackie seemed more at home with the gossip than he was. "Are they really separating?" He could not imagine Meg and Alan apart from each other.

"They say they are," said Jackie. "And they're pretending it's all good, clean fun. But *my* sources, of which I have one, say they really want to kill each other, and they're waiting till after Christmas to fight about who gets how much. New Year's the traditional time for murder, isn't it?"

"Do you know the Kilmers?" asked Ellis.

"Never met them until five minutes ago," said Jackie.

Ellis came to a sudden stop. "Just level with me—what are we *doing* here?" he asked. "Why have we crashed this particular party?"

"Well, to tell you the truth, I want to make trouble,"

said Jackie. "I didn't mention it before, in case you got all shy, but . . ." He tilted his head back and drank the whole glass of beer in what seemed to be a single swallow. "Don't *you* do that!" he added. "Remember, you're driving."

"What sort of trouble?" asked Ellis dubiously.

"I'm still *choosing*," said Jackie in a pious voice. Then his gaze sharpened, and he stared past Ellis with an expression of such deep appreciation that Ellis turned, too. And there he saw his childhood nemesis, the Kilmer boy, Christo, talking to a lanky young woman wearing jeans, a sleeveless blue top, and round, wire-rimmed glasses.

6:55 P.M. – FRIDAY

Ellis and Christo had never got on together, though both sets of parents had tried hard to encourage them into some sort of friendship. In normal circumstances Ellis would have gone a long way to avoid talking to Christo. But Jackie was drifting so casually in his and the girl's direction that nobody watching him would have guessed how purposeful that drifting was. Only Ellis knew—and suddenly knew for certain—that Jackie had forced his way into this party with the single intention of breaking in on *that* particular conversation. Ellis had no choice but to follow him, though with increasing alarm.

The couple had been chatting together cheerfully enough, or so it seemed to Ellis. Now Christo, looking across the girl's shoulder, met Ellis's eyes, and then, almost instantaneously, saw Jackie. Though Jackie was still pretending he had not yet seen Christo, Ellis felt the impact of Christo's furious glance as if a dagger had been thrust toward them. Even from where he stood he could see Christo's fair skin turn red as a wild blush of fury spread across it. A small mole, rather like an eighteenth-century beauty spot, stood out darkly on Christo's cheekbone as he grasped the girl's upper arm. Christo's grasp must have been severe, for she started, glanced at him, then turned in order to see what he was looking at. For a moment, she was as amazed as Jackie could ever have wished her to be. Behind her wire-rimmed glasses, under the shadow of her lashes, her eyes were a light, startling blue. Her first surprise gave way to instant anger. "What are *you* doing here?" she shouted.

Jackie looked directly at her for the first time. His expression showed nothing but startled innocence. "Oh, wow!" he exclaimed. "You! What a coincidence! Hey, it's a small world, isn't it? Stunted, really."

"What are you doing here?" she repeated so forcefully that Ellis stepped back in alarm.

"Weird, eh?" Jackie went on. "Must be the morphic field! Or what's that other thing? Chaos theory or something! See, I met up with Ellis—my old friend Ellis—you know, I'm always talking about Ellis—and he suggested—"

"You're such a liar!" exclaimed the girl.

Jackie laughed. "Ellis," he said. "This is Ursa Hammond. And you know Chris, don't you?"

"Christo!" Christo corrected him. He had always hated it when people called him "Chris."

"Oh! Sorry!" said Jackie, returning the hostility with his wide, innocent smile. "Hey, your parents know how to celebrate failure in style. Great party."

People always said how handsome Christo was. Even though Ellis had detested him for a long time, and so much so that he thought of him as essentially disfigured, he was fair-minded enough to admit they were right.

"What are you *doing* here?" Christo was demanding, suddenly as furious as his companion, though Ellis understood there was a great difference between their two angers.

"Doing here?" repeated Jackie, frowning. "Big question. But what are any of us doing here, if it comes to that? I reckon it's pretty random myself. What's that word you were going on about the other day?" he asked, turning to Ursa. "Not telepathy, but *like* telepathy. It was to do with design or something . . . that things keep happening because of what's meant to happen."

"Teleology," said Ursa. Ellis thought he could hear her first anger laced with some other mood as Jackie ran on and on, shaking his head in wonder. She was recognizing something in Jackie and was unwillingly entertained by it. "Leave it alone, Jackie! Bug off!" she muttered.

"Nobody wants you here," said Christo, provoked exactly as Jackie intended him to be provoked. He turned to Ellis. "Why the hell are you hanging out with this shit?"

Ellis looked directly at Christo for the first time.

Many years ago, before Ellis could swim properly, Christo and his sister, Sophie, had pushed him into a deep pool down among the willows and, with chilly interest, had watched him gasping and choking, struggling and sinking, pushing him under again and again with their bare feet, only pulling him out at what might have been his very last minute. They had then threatened him with terrible pain if he told either his parents or theirs. They also told him they had drowned kittens and puppies in that very pool. Ellis found that he still hated Christo, with hatred as fresh and tender as if it had just been born in him. Watching Jackie dance around Christo, as he himself had never been able to do, filled him with hot pleasure.

"I just dropped in to say 'Hi!'" he said, his voice as innocent as Jackie's. "And then your mom invited us to stay." He sensed Jackie turn to him as if they were practiced cross-talk comedians putting on a show they had rehearsed over and over again.

"Your mom clapped eyes on us and knew we were the right stuff," Jackie said to Christo, but then he began filling his beer glass from the bottle of red wine. Ellis watched the level rise with incredulity. "She invited us to eat and drink all we could."

"Well, I'm inviting you to get *out*," said Christo. "I suppose *Ellis* can stay if he wants to," he said, emphasizing Ellis's name with casual contempt. "But not you! Get out before I sling you out."

The girl made a sudden sharp move, and Jackie, holding the mug of red wine in front of him, gave an odd, gasping laugh.

"You and whose army, mate?" he asked, smiling down into the wine. "You and whose army?" He looked up, and Ellis found Jackie had suddenly become alarming, though all he had done was widen his eyes a little and fasten them intently on Christo. Christo, who had stepped forward confidently, hesitated.

"Oh, no!" cried Ursa sharply. She glanced first at Jackie's bare feet and then at Ellis. "You've got a car? You must have."

"Back in the drive," Ellis admitted.

"Just go and stand beside it and wait for me," she said. "My sister's here, too. I'll find her, and we'll be with you in a moment. You go with him," she added, looking briefly at Jackie.

"Jesus! *You* don't have to go," exclaimed Christo, sounding desperate. "For God's sake, Ursie . . . you're a *guest. Invited!* Do you think I can't cope with this deadbeat? I can easily manage him. I've done it a thousand times."

"Manage me?" said Jackie vaguely. He bunched his right-hand fingers together and tapped them against the center of his forehead, frowning. "Was that at school? Wish I could remember! Brain damage, maybe."

A few nearby partygoers, catching on to an interesting argument, were watching curiously. Ellis gave them a placating smile, trying to suggest it was all good fun.

Jackie now drank half the mug of wine without a moment's hesitation. He smiled and wiped his hand across his mouth. "A superior little wine," he said. "A lovely, voluptuous grape!"

"Christo, I'm sorry," Ursa was saying as she moved away "But just look around you. Everyone's being so civilized . . . and it's nearly Christmas. What'll your parents think if you suddenly have a punch-up at their party?"

"They'll blame me," said Christo. "They're a couple of selfish shits, and they always blame me."

"Oh, no! They'll blame *me,*" said Ursa. "They might even blame Leo! No, thanks!"

And she began to hurry toward the steps that led to the upper lawn. Forgetting Jackie, Christo set off after her, almost leaping beside her, apparently trying to argue her into staying. Ellis had never seen Christo so desperate–so vulnerable–before.

"I hate that bastard," said Jackie cheerfully. He drank the rest of the red wine as if it were orange juice. "He's suffering, though, isn't he? Good!"

"Be fair: his parents, his party!" said Ellis lightly, doing his best to sound like a disinterested watcher making a point. "What's-her-name–Ursa–is she your girl or something?"

"She's something," said Jackie. "Not a girlfriend! Not *as such*! But she's not going to be his, either."

"So what's the story, since you're writing the plot?" asked Ellis.

"Ursie's gone to find her sister. You race over and curtsy to the hostess. Do you think she'll mind me walking out with a few nutritious scraps and a bottle of wine?"

Ellis looked around. He saw meat cooling beside the barbecue, and other bottles of wine half empty and already looking abandoned.

Jackie, sighing deeply and shaking his head like a man being forced to violate his own better judgment, poured one half-bottle of wine into another. "Red and white makes pink," he said. "I love bad taste. Love it!" Then he jammed a cork into the neck of the bottle and slid it into one of his deep pockets.

"Innocent grapes *died* so we could have this wine," he went on. "They were crushed, mashed to a pulp. Anyhow, when I was a kid I had to eat everything put in front of me."

Ellis set off, crossing first one lawn, then climbing the stone steps to the other, Jackie bounding beside him. They went back round the house, past the garage, and waited, side by side, in the soft darkness under the chestnut trees.

"What's it all about, anyway?" asked Ellis.

But Jackie did not answer. It was too dim in the shadow of the chestnuts to make out his precise expression, but somehow Ellis believed it would be both sinister and sad. At some time in the past, Ellis suddenly knew for certain, Jackie had also suffered at the un-kind, confident hands of Christo Kilmer.

"I can't stand him, either," he said.

"No one can," said Jackie. "It's starting to drive him round the bend. But, hey–that's the right place for him. He'll meet himself coming the other way."

They waited while the sound of voices rose from beyond the brick angles of the house, and the smell of the barbecue settled insistently around them. One voice suddenly sounded closer than the others. Ellis looked sideways down the drive toward the house. Quite unprepared for what was about to happen to him, he was overwhelmed by a vision.

Passing through the moving patches of light that shifted uneasily in the curving drive was a girl he knew he was seeing for the first time in his life. All the same, it now seemed to Ellis that for months–maybe even years–he had been expecting to see this very girl, mov-ing from darkness into light and then back into dark-ness again as she came toward him, her hair flaring, then fading, brightening sharply, before growing shad-owy once again. She was wearing a very short skirt. Her legs were exquisite. They swept her toward him, and she spoke as she came, but not to Ellis. It was Jackie she had recognized.

"Oh, Jackie! Ursie says you're ruining things for us."

"Gee, she's bright!" said Jackie. "It must be all that law she studies."

"She's not keen on Christo, if that's what you're afraid of," the girl said. "She just wanted to go to a big party." Her voice was soft, a little plaintive perhaps, but also amused.

"But life's a continual big party back in the Land-of-Smiles!" said Jackie, talking, Ellis supposed, the sort of nonsense well understood between friends. He and Simon had once had a private nonsense language that excluded everyone else. Come to think of it, that private language was one of the things Ellis missed most—now that Simon was dead.

"It's nothing but parties in the Land-of-Smiles," Jackie persisted.

"Not big parties like this one," the girl replied. "Our parties are all scruffy and disgusting."

"No such thing as a scruffy undertaker," said Jackie, indulging once again in the language of private reference. He turned suddenly. "Ellis, this is Leo Hammond. Leona! Leona the Lion! Leo, this is Ellis. Okay?"

Then Ursa was coming down the drive toward them, almost jogging, with Christo still skirmishing around her, arguing and gesticulating on one side, then leaping to the other, as if hearing his arguments with a different ear might make her change her mind. When he saw Ellis and Jackie watching him, he grabbed Ursa's arm, forcing her to stop. Then they kissed—or perhaps he kissed her. It was hard to be sure.

"Bor-ing!" said Jackie, yawning. But for all that, he suddenly sounded not angry, exactly, but certainly petulant.

7:30 P.M.—FRIDAY

Ursa climbed into the passenger seat beside Ellis and sat there in silence. Jackie opened the back door and slid in to recline gracefully along most of the backseat. Leona followed him. It was Ellis's car, but he felt as if he did not exist for any of them except as a sort of driving ghost. All space in the car was taken over by the argument between Jackie and the angular Ursa, even though, in the beginning, the argument was conducted in silence.

"Shift over!" Leona said. "You're such a pain, Jackie."

"Home, James!" Jackie called triumphantly, pointing across Ellis's shoulder.

Ellis started the car, wishing that Leona, rather than Ursa, were sitting beside him. Before he could stop himself, he was imagining light shifting on her rounded knees, outlining them in the darkness that lurked below the glove compartment of his mother's car.

37

"You know," said Ursa, half turning to glare at Jackie, "I was having a really nice time. Not wonderful! Not thrilling! Just nice! Instead of sitting around with a lot of screwed-up no-hopers, I was in a beautiful place with a beautiful garden, and I was enjoying talking to Christo and drinking champagne."

"Some champagne!" said Jackie scornfully. "Made right here in New Zealand."

"It did well in a competition in France," said Ursa. "It came first—or almost first."

"Second, say," Jackie suggested. "Or third!"

"Don't sit in the back, cuddling the bottle. You look disgusting," said Ursa. "And don't try to make out *you*'ve got taste of any kind," she added. "You'd cuddle up to cat's piss as long as it was free."

"You bet I would," Jackie agreed. "Cat's piss has a delicate, crisp acidity, shot through with suggestions of grubby earthiness, the flavor of gooseberries mixed with a tang of acetone. It has a chunky chewiness to it that—"

But Ursa raised her voice and talked over him. "And don't think you can joke your way out of this, Jackie. You purposefully set out to ruin things for me. You just hate to think I might drift away from the Land-of-Smiles, don't you?"

Ellis, having driven between the chestnut trees, was turning out onto the road once more.

"Forget it, Ursie," said Leona's soft voice. "You'll say something awful—something you'll be sorry for. Or *he* will!"

"I don't need him acting like a sort of Big Daddy," Ursa cried impatiently.

"Well, I promise not to act like *yours,* anyway," said Jackie, and Ellis could hear a sudden ferocious nudge in his voice—a peculiar emphasis twisting the ordinary words.

There was a sudden silence—a silence far more violent than the argument had been. Something had been said that changed the whole nature of the quarrel . . . something unforgivable. Ellis longed to check out their expressions, but dared not take his eyes from the road. The car seemed to speed up, almost independently of his foot on the accelerator. Signs announcing that the highway was a mere kilometer away rushed toward them.

"Okay," commanded Ursa in an icy voice. "Stop the car! Stop right now!"

"Oh, no!" cried Leona. "He didn't mean it, Ursie. You know he can't resist a smart answer."

"Stop!" yelled Ursa so fiercely that Ellis braked sharply, and Leona fell silent. "I want to say something to that . . . *thing* in the back, and it's not safe to say it in a moving car."

Ellis brought the car to a graceful standstill. Ursa turned under the strap of her seat belt and stared at Jackie—slumped behind her, eating, insolently eating, a sausage stolen from the barbecue.

"Get out!" Ursa said.

"What?" said Jackie, surprised at last, looking at her obliquely across the half-eaten sausage.

"Ursie!" groaned Leona. "It's only making it worse."

"Ursie! Ursie! Don't make it worse-ie!" sang Jackie mockingly.

Ursa ignored her sister. "Get out of this car," she repeated. "I don't want to breathe the same air as you."

"You're going to dump me on the side of the road?" Jackie cried, sitting bolt upright, and making his voice deliberately pathetic. "How am I going to get home?" His voice was thickening a little. Words ran into one another. "And I'm beginning to get drunk, too," he added accusingly, as if it were Ursa's fault.

"Walk!" she commanded.

"You mean, 'skate!'" said Jackie. "I've got my Rollerblades and–"

"Okay! Skate, mate!" she said. "Because if you don't get out, I will."

"Yeah, but maybe you've made some arrangement with Chris–oh, sorry! I should have said 'Christ' since that's who he thinks he is," Jackie said, making a rude gesture with the sausage. "Maybe he'll come along in that new red car and–"

"Are you scared?" asked Ursa scornfully. "Frightened he'll run you down?"

"He just might," said Jackie. "He was the official school bully . . . got a cup for it at the end-of-school breakup, didn't he, Ellis? A silver cup with handles and–"

"He could be a bit rough," agreed Ellis.

"Get out!" said Ursa to Jackie.

"Oh, Ursa, leave him alone," cried Leona. "He said what he said. You can't change anything."

"Look, I can't just dump Jackie," Ellis cut in, protesting.

"Then dump *me*," Ursa cried. She opened her door and pushed one foot out into the darkness.

"No!" yelled Jackie. "No! I don't care. Take her home, Ellis. I'll skate. I'll hitch. I'll probably get there before you."

Ursa slammed her door shut.

"Get where?" asked Ellis.

"She'll tell you where," said Jackie. "She's good at laying down the law."

A back door slammed. Then Ursa opened her door again. Ellis thought that perhaps she had relented. But she was only throwing the Rollerblades out after Jackie. "Drive!" said Ursa. "Please," she added.

"What did he say that was so bad?" Ellis asked.

"Oh, it's a long story," Ursa replied. "He's sorry now, but that's not enough. I want him to suffer."

As the car moved off, Ellis saw through the back window Jackie's shape, picked out in the red glow of the taillight, apparently giving a thumbs-up sign with one hand, and hoisting the bottle with the other. . . .

"He's drunk a lot," Ellis said doubtfully. "He might flake out."

"I hope he does," said Ursa. "It's not as if I give a

41

stuff about Christopher Kilmer. I know he's a bit of a creep—sorry, if he's a friend of yours, but—"

"He isn't a friend," said Ellis shortly.

"It's just as if I'm being punished for wanting to have a good time," Ursa complained. "I need it, too. Anyone needs a good time if their computer's just been stolen, which mine was, last night."

Ellis found he was beginning to remember Ursa vaguely from the days before he went to Saint Conan's. In his head, a past version had begun flicking on and off like an inconstant ghost—shorter and fatter than she was now, and wearing glasses that had black tape wrapped around one of the side pieces. She had been a loud girl, he now remembered, always talking—the skirt of her school uniform hitched up over her belt so that it looked much shorter than the regulation length. She must have been wondering about him, too.

"I thought I knew everyone Jackie knew," she said, turning her powerful gaze toward him.

"I've been out of town. Studying!" Ellis quickly added. He did not want Leona to know that only yesterday he had been at school.

"Studying what?" Ursa asked.

"General stuff," said Ellis. He was irritated by her skeptical voice. "What about you?" he asked, glad to hear himself sounding mildly aggressive.

"Law!" she replied absently, but not as if she were really interested in letting him know. "Law and philosophy. I need the philosophy right this minute, and I'll need the law a little later on."

8:10 P.M.*— FRIDAY*

Ellis, doing what he was told to do, left the highway on a different road from the one by which he had entered. He found himself driving past lawns and mailboxes and deserted shopping centers, one of a number of cars that seemed uncertain quite where they wanted to go. Ellis recognized the names of suburbs without knowing exactly where he was in the changing city.

"Right at these lights!" commanded Ursa. "Straight on for a couple of blocks, then right again." Ellis turned obediently into a wide avenue, lined on either side with well-established plane trees, and became part of a continuous line of cars. They were back in the center of the city. He knew where he was. He would be home in half an hour.

Yet, just as he was relaxing and beginning to feel in charge of life once more, the city gave him an unexpected jolt that, almost at once, changed into the feeling that what he was seeing had first come out of his own head. Houses on the left gave way to a floodlit slope of neatly cut grass; oaks framed a chaste, white building. It was gently lit and glowed in the summer twilight. DOMMETT & CHRISTIE, said a notice, cool, plain, discreet, but clearly visible. INTEGRITY FUNERALS. It seemed he could not escape—might never escape—from Simon's ironic smile, for Dommett & Christie had organized Simon's funeral. After his death, Simon's body had been taken to this white building, and someone somewhere in there had given him a final, enigmatic expression.

Ellis had not realized just how changeable Simon's living expression had been until, in the chapel at the crematorium, he found himself face-to-face with a stillness fixed forever by the skill of an undertaker . . . the suggestion of a smile about to begin but never quite beginning. Had there possibly been just a little *smugness* about that last expression? It was almost as if, in some *dead* way, Simon knew he had finally upstaged Ellis— had pulled off an act that could never be surpassed. As he thought this Ellis's hands tightened on the wheel, while his own voice repeated in his head:

> " . . . 'tis too horrible.
> *The weariest and most loathed worldly life*
> *That age, ache, penury, and imprisonment*
> *Can lay on nature is a paradise*
> *To what we fear of death."*

"Home sweet home," said Leona a little wearily, interrupting his thoughts.

"Well, almost!" said Ursa. "Turn right into Moncrieff Street. Here!" she added, though Ellis had already recognized Moncrieff Street, one of the oldest streets in the city. These days it was part of the grid of one-way streets around the city center. Ellis saw a white sheet with words painted on it fastened across the window of a darkened shop. PARTY! LAND-OF-SMILES! said the blue letters, rough but clear. Ursa groaned. "Did you see that?" she said to Leona. "Can't I go out for an evening without . . ."

But now they were skirting the Moncrieff Street cemetery, a historic landmark. Tall, and sometimes broken, gravestones rose, like pale, admonishing fingers from beyond a low, stone wall. Someone had sprayed the words ANARCHY RULES, OKAY? on the stones—possibly one of the three children in baggy clothes briefly seen as they darted up a path and into the darkness under old trees.

"The glue gang!" Ursa said in the absentminded voice of someone checking off landmarks as she returned to familiar territory. "Is Terry Stamp still hanging out with Jason these days?" She asked this question without seeming to expect any answer. "Three blocks down and turn to the left," she added, speaking directly to Ellis this time. "It's a skinny little street—Garden Lane—so don't drive too fast and miss it."

High in the city air, a bright sign flashed on and off. A blond woman was beckoning with a jerking arm, swinging one bare leg out and back, out and back. Her scarlet mouth widened in a smile, then shrank back into a pursed, electric kiss. Ellis drove toward this spasmodic beauty. Beneath her jittering leg was a lighted doorway through which people were either coming or going. And then they were past her, cruising between two lines of largely darkened shop windows. IT'S NEVER TOO LATE FOR BREAKFAST, said a flashing sign. THE SOUTHERN GRENADIER, proclaimed another sign—old, square lettering across the front of a grimy hotel.

"There! Turn there!" said Ursa, pointing.

Ellis turned the car yet again, this time into a narrow street crowded with houses that were not only old but were visibly disintegrating. The lingering twilight, which had seemed so pure out in the country, had taken on a smeared and grubby quality. On either side he saw rusting roofs, broken fences, and gateposts guarded by long grasses.

"And now to the left again. It's really a right-of-way for pedestrians . . . but people don't mind if you drive along it. Take it easy, though!"

Everything around them was so shabby that Ellis felt conscious of the shine on his mother's car. A long, low building shaped like the letter "E" with its middle stroke missing seemed to advance wearily through the twilight. Colored letters flashed in the air above it. A stream of scarlet, electric arrows leaped like frightened fish, arching over and emphasizing the blue and green letters below. THE AND OF MILES, announced the sign. There was no gate and no fence. LAND-OF-SMILES MOTEL, a second dingy sign elaborated at the gate in letters rather more reliable than the electric ones.

"Home sweet home." It was Ursa who spoke this time. "Look, thanks for bringing us back, and sorry about all the complications. Like a cup of coffee, after all that?"

Ellis hesitated. In the silence he heard rackety music beating in from somewhere.

"Do come!" said Leona. "It sounds as if we've got a houseful already, but we can find a peaceful place somewhere."

"The gang's here!" said Ursa gloomily. "As always!"

Ellis almost said that he'd better be getting home—indeed, he'd been thinking of home with pleasure—and yet, within a breath, the words he was shaping in the back of his mouth twisted on his tongue, and came out saying something that surprised him much more than they surprised anyone else.

"Great! Okay to leave the car here?" After all, in spite of everything that had happened, it was still early. Not even half past eight, yet.

"Safer than some places," Ursa said, smiling and sketching the sign of the cross in the air with her finger.

8:25 P.M.—FRIDAY

Following Ursa and Leona in through the front door, Ellis was immediately aware that the Land-of-Smiles Motel, though it was no longer used as a motel, was haunted by its past. He was confronted by a small counter, across the front of which narrow ledges and sagging, rusting wires had once supported brochures and flyers advertising city tours. A phone stood on the end of the counter, a phone book beside it, and the wall beside the phone was scribbled and scratched with a swarm of numbers, some of them boxed in so that they could be easily found again. Leaning against a wall beyond the counter was the sort of backpack used for carrying a small child, an unexpectedly innocent object in such weary surroundings.

Behind the counter was a door, and it was from behind this door that music was forcing its way out. And now Ellis could also hear voices shouting, not because

48

they were angry, but because the music was so very loud that people had to shout to make themselves heard.

"Why did we bother to leave home?" asked Leona.

"I wanted style," said Ursa. "I deserve it." She opened the door and strode into the gale of sound.

Leona turned, smiling and gesturing at Ellis. "Come on," she shouted.

The room into which she led him must once have been a dining room. Tables piled on top of one another took up almost a quarter of it. But three tables, at least, were still in use, pushed end to end to make one long, lopsided table around which people were sitting, yelling over the music. Ellis, dazed by the sound, glimpsed, between the feet of about a dozen dancers, a roaring tape deck.

Looking over Leona's shoulder, past the sweep of her shining hair, Ellis saw one particular face, mouth working as its owner made some inaudible announcement. This face was tattooed on the chin and cheeks with Maori designs, though the face seemed pakeha (European) in every other way. But another face–the one turned toward the tattoos–had its own insignia. It glittered. Ears, nostrils, and eyebrows glinted with rings. The gesturing hands, also covered in rings, seemed more like metallic robot hands than those of an ordinary man.

"Hello, folks!" yelled Ursa. "Here we are again."

There was a ragged, derisive chorus–derisive but also affectionate, Ellis thought. A few hands shot up; a few faces lifted and grinned. But neither shouting nor music abated. Only the glittering man seemed really aware of them, and he shook his head while wagging a ringed forefinger from side to side as if he were canceling Ursa's words out of existence. The man on his right, and the girl on his left, both reached for cans of beer as if suddenly remembering that it was their duty to drink everything within reach.

Ursa took Ellis's arm, her thin, strong fingers tightening just above his elbow. She pulled him across the room toward yet another door, then through it into a big kitchen. The door closed behind them. The music, though it could not be shut out, was at least held at bay.

Even the kitchen was already occupied. Just inside the door a gray-haired man leaned back in a carved throne of a chair—a chair so tall and wide that it dwarfed him, making the rest of the room seem slightly out of proportion, like a doll's house kitchen, carefully made but still not quite right. The man had a book open on his knee, though Ellis doubted if he could possibly be reading it. It was a prop of some kind . . . a way of pointing out that he, the apparent reader, had a mind that reached beyond the mindless confusion around him.

"Monty, this is Ellis," Leona said. "Ellis, this is Lewis Montgomery . . . a sort of guardian of ours from way back."

"They're more like *my* guardians these days," Monty said, and smiled with a sweetness that seemed simultaneously to be a form of profound bitterness. "You turned out to be a sound investment, Ursie."

"Don't you forget it, either," said Ursa.

"She should be in bed," Leona cried, bending over beside the chair. "Lewis, you promised."

And when she straightened, Ellis saw she was holding a small child of less than a year, not much more than a baby. "She shouldn't be crawling around at this time of night." Leona was looking far more concerned than she had been over anything Christo or Jackie had said or done . . . far more concerned than she had been at having to leave the Kilmers' party so unexpectedly.

Monty smiled again, rather patronizingly this time. "She was crying in her cot," he said. "The Orono Indians never leave children crying."

"You and the Orono Indians!" said Leona, sounding amused but irritated. The child stared at Ellis with huge, dark eyes, hair sticking up in tufts like a fringe of white silk.

"They have a highly successful community," Monty said with a kind of fluting smugness. "No crime! No broken families."

"She's okay, that's the main thing," said Ursa, ignoring Monty and smiling at the baby. "Hey, Ellis—see that blue can over there? Bring it down and open it."

"Do you *live* here?" Ellis asked, half turning to Leona. He was horrified to hear how shocked he sounded.

Ursa laughed. "If you can call it living," she said. "It's humble—but, hey!—it's home."

Pulling down the blue can as he had been directed, Ellis opened it and found it full of homemade short-bread. Ursa reached over and took a piece. Holding it between her teeth, she opened the refrigerator and located a packet of coffee from the freezer compartment.

"Help yourself!" she mumbled, her mouth full of shortbread as she began measuring coffee into a cof-feepot with a plunger.

Somewhere to his left, a door opened. Turning, Ellis looked for a moment into a narrow, dark yard filled with trash bags, and along a line of identical windows, marking what seemed to be a series of rooms, apparently attached in some way to the kitchen. Then the door closed, the view disappeared, and, lowering his gaze a little, Ellis found himself confronting a sharp-faced child of about twelve, wearing not one but two drifting black shawls draped over striped pajamas. Her fair hair was held in two ragged bunches that stuck out sideways over her ears, and her hands were clasped across something like a bleeding heart, apparently forcing its way out of her chest. There was, however, no distress in her watchful expression. She looked like a familiar spirit coming out of the shadows.

9:30 P.M. — FRIDAY

"**Hi**, Foxie," said Ursa. "Ellis, this is my sister, Fox. Fox, this is Ellis . . . Ellis . . ." She looked at him uncertainly. "Ellis Someone," she said at last. "He rescued me from the party and drove me home."

Fox stood looking from one to the other of them with sharp assessment. Someone crashed against the door of the dining room while voices roared with what sounded like applause. Monty sighed and leaned back in his big chair. He picked up his book again, assuming it like a disguise. Ellis wondered if he carried it around with him all the time, automatically opening it during moments of crisis. Beside him, Leona cuddled the baby. Ellis could not remember seeing anything more beautiful, and unexpectedly sexy, than her tenderness. When they left the room, the child looking back at them across her shoulder, he stared after her as if she were a vanishing light.

"I thought you wanted to go," Fox was saying to Ursa, rather accusingly. "You said you'd really enjoy a good yuppie barbecue."

"It was great," said Ursa. "I was just so turned on by it all. Yup! Yup! Yup! There I was with a good-looking guy–well, okay, he's as thick as old custard but he's a bit of a stud for all that–long eyelashes, great haircut, *and* a beauty spot, as well. Anyhow, there I was, eating wonderful steak and salad, and drinking red wine–*good* red wine, not just cheap stuff from a cask. And then, guess who turned up and ruined everything?"

Fox looked sideways at Ellis. "Him?" she said, puzzled but smiling, and seeming to know already that Ellis could not possibly ruin anything for anyone.

"Just think of the most embarrassing big-mouth we know . . . ," said Ursa, holding up an instructional finger.

Fox's face suddenly flared into life. She grinned from ear to ear. "Jackie?" she cried, then clapped one hand across her mouth, as if some terrible oath had slipped through her unguarded lips.

"Jackie!" Ursa nodded her head. "Bloody Jackie. He'd exploited Ellis here into giving him a lift (I don't know how) and–oh, man–he was perfectly prepared to make trouble. So there it was! I'd hit the big time, and suddenly there was my"–she stopped and made a face–"well, not my past . . . a bit of another sort of present, really . . . another *dimension* . . . swilling down the red wine as if it were water, just to prove he wasn't weighed down by good taste."

"He *tells* you he isn't," said Fox.

54

"There's no need for him to go to so much trouble to prove it over and over again," Ursa replied.

What *is* this place? Ellis was thinking. "What is this place?" he now said aloud. The most personal thing in the kitchen was a calendar, featuring various celebrities and their dogs, pinned to the wall beside the door. Ellis had seen it earlier in the year in other houses, looking far more natural than it possibly could in this room, for the pictures suggested family life and affectionate pet ownership, and nothing he had seen so far in the Land-of-Smiles matched up. This kitchen was a public space in which one might make a cup of tea or eat fish-and-chips before rushing on to the next thing. The Formica countertops, though a little smeary, were clean, but the top of the stove was crowded with pots that looked as if they had lived there for years and had nowhere else to go. The windows and windowsills and the edges of the kitchen shelves looked grubby, not with any really noticeable dirt, but because a particular sort of carelessness had laid itself down on them for year after year . . . an established, stratified neglect. Whoa! Ellis ordered himself, closing his eyes, annoyed by his own dismay. Now was the time to say a polite good-bye and make for home. But wouldn't that good-bye be rather like walking out before the end of the film? And, besides, he wanted to see Leona just once more.

"Starting a fight is all Jackie's good for," Fox was saying scornfully. "At present!" she added mysteriously, smirking at Ellis, who could now see that her hands were clasped, not over a bleeding heart but over a ball of red glass that glowed between her thin fingers. Holding it out stiffly in front of her, she peered into its crimson depths. Her eyes crossed slightly as she stared at it, apparently reading a message hidden from everyone else. Ellis saw the ball reflected in her eyes, rather as if the pupils had turned to drops of blood. "It's going to change," she chanted. "The glass shows all!"

And immediately Ursa seemed to change—to change her opinion, at least. "Oh, Jackie's good for a lot more than starting fights," she cried. "I'm not saying he isn't a deadbeat, because he is. But he's not stupid. Those clever parents of his just don't catch on to his sort of cleverness. It's an *inside* cleverness. And, any-how, he doesn't start fights. He just drives other people to start them."

"You slag him off all the time, so I can, too," Fox replied.

"No, you can't!" said Ursa. "I'm the only one who is allowed to take a crack at Jack!"

"And you'll win out," said Fox, deliberately mak-ing her voice weird. "It's wri-i-itten in the gla-a-ass! A finger of fire is setting it down."

Ursa laughed. "Yeah! Yeah! The glass tells all," she said, nodding and sounding as if she were responding to a ritual line. "You're the magician of the family."

And then she caught Ellis's eye and looked a little surprised to find he was still there. "Sorry!" she said. "You're being neglected."

"What is this place?" Ellis asked.

"Home!" Ursa answered. "You brought me home."

"It used to be a motel," said Fox. "Monty . . . our guardian, Monty–"

"He's met Monty," Ursa put in, and they all looked toward Monty, who vaguely waved his book at them, though he did not look up. "Monty bought it a few years ago and he takes in paying guests–"

"They don't *pay,*" Fox objected.

"Well! Okay! They just doss down for the duration," said Ursa. "Most of them rip us off, but they do it in a golden-hearted way. And some of them *do* pay, Foxie. Be fair!" She grinned at Ellis. "At least none of them have beaten us up so far."

"I like to think of this place as a refuge," said Monty to Ellis.

"And they eat our stuff," added Fox, settling herself at the table, placing the glass ball in front of her and cupping her hands around it as if it were giving off warmth. "They just help themselves from the fridge."

"And to other people's computers," said Ursa. "Monty–over there in the big chair–our Monty used to work for the Department of Social Welfare. But then he retired–"

"He was *struck off,*" said Fox with a long, dark smile curiously echoed in her blue eyes. "He had sex with a girl who was only fifteen," she cried with something like relish.

Behind them, Monty sighed. "Don't mind my

feelings," he said wearily. "I loved her . . . I *loved* her . . . but nobody ever mentions that."

"She was fifteen going on thirty-seven, poor kid," Ursa said. "And poor Monty, too." She ruffled his hair, but he pushed her hand away. "Now, let that lot sink in for"—she looked at her watch—"seven and a half minutes and then ask another question. More coffee?"

"He hasn't had any yet, so he can't have more," said Fox, and then both sisters spoke together in a ragged chorus.

"It's very easy to have more than nothing," they cried, and then they laughed together.

Ellis did not know what to say to any of this. It sounded familiar, almost Shakespearean. He was sure, however, that the words weren't from any of the plays he had studied. As he tried to remember where he had heard them before, he met the eyes of the youngest sister, and found them alight with unexpected expression—with recognition. She was staring at him as if they were old friends meeting again after a long separation. But then, before Ellis had time to be disconcerted by this strange, knowing regard, the door through which Fox had come into the kitchen flew open once more, and three men staggered through, all laughing. A strong smell of alcohol blew in around them.

"Oh, no! Not you lot!" said Ursa with amused disgust. "Hey, listen! Somebody pinched my computer last night. It wasn't one of you, was it?" A dark, middle-aged man with tattooed hands toppled toward her, flinging his arms around her shoulders in an embrace. "Strange, dear, but true, dear . . . ," he sang in a husky, melodious voice, and they danced a few steps together, still laughing, while one of the other men sank down in a corner, saying, "Somebody pinched your computer. *Your* computer? He'll probably get accident compensation."

"Everyone slings off at my computer," said Ursa protestingly. "But I knew how to use it. It had a lot of my stuff on it."

"Whoever took it was sure as hell one dude who didn't know his Microsoft from his hard drive," cried the man in the corner.

"Where's this party?" the third man interrupted. "Oh, God–is that coffee?" he added, and made for the plunger.

"No! No!" cried Fox, defending the plunger as she waved vaguely at Ellis, who had first rights to the coffee. The man in the corner held up a bottle toward Ellis, which he accepted. He lifted it halfway to his mouth, then hesitated.

"Drink away! We haven't got AIDS," said the tattooed man. "Not yet!" he added, and began to laugh. Terrified at the thought of seeming standoffish, Ellis drank without even looking at the label.

"Danny, Prince, and Harley," Ursa was shouting. "Meet Ellis . . . Ellis Someone."

"Oh, yeah?" said the man in the corner. "One of the famous Someone family. Me, too! We're related, bro!"

Next door the music was suddenly blotted out by human voices yelling, not singing. The sound came toward the kitchen like the grumble of an approaching earthquake, bursting out from under and around the door. It must have vibrated in the wall as well, for the calendar trembled and then fell to the floor. Ellis took a step back, ready to make for the second door and run off, if necessary. But nobody else seemed to be paying much attention. The voices began to subside, and the music took over once more. Kitchen conversations began again. Ursa, noting Ellis's alarm, shook her head at him.

"Don't ask!" she shouted, having to raise her voice to be heard. "And anyhow, everything that can be broken out there has already been broken." Ellis tried to force himself to relax, smiling what he hoped was a worldly smile. Then the door to the yard swung wide again, and a young woman with curly red hair looked in at them, smiling, as if she knew she would be welcome. Behind her stood Jackie, tall on his Rollerblades, and beaming triumphantly. Kitchen light caressed the trash bags beyond him.

"Told you I'd hitch a ride!" he said clearly enough, although his voice now had a decided edge of incoherence. "Catherine saw me skating along the edge of the highway, deserted by my so-called friends." He looked around him with pleasure. "Did you know someone had stuck up an open invitation to a party here up at the top of Moncrieff Street?" And he flourished a plastic bag holding half a dozen cold sausages in his right hand while his left waved an unopened bottle that Ellis recognized as Kilmer wine. But, from that moment on, Ellis, himself, began to lose his grip on the world.

TIME STOPS

He drank his second glass of wine rather more quickly than he had drunk the first, and then someone passed him an unidentified drink that, recklessly, he tossed down.

Time stopped.

Entrenched in some timeless inner space, he watched the two doors open, close, open again—and, finally, remain open. Suddenly, there were people everywhere, talking, shouting, gesturing. He saw Ursa taking Fox by the shoulders to push her, protesting, toward bed.

But by then Ellis himself was talking to Harley, the man gloved with tattoos, who was directing him on to yet another tattooed man, the man he had seen earlier . . . the man with the Maori patterns on his cheeks, blue lines spiraling tightly across planes so hard and unyielding that the lines seemed part of a graffitied wall rather than the decoration of a live, human face. The words DRUGS! BOOZE! SEX! marched across his forehead. Thick, gray hair was pulled back in a tight ponytail. Looking with wonder at this man, Ellis encountered an inexplicably calculating stare. He thought he detected resentment in it, as if, simply by being there, he had somehow issued a challenge.

"Phipps!" said the man, holding out a hand inscribed with words and pictures. "Put it there!" And Ellis did put it there, aware of the way his own plain thumb stood out against the intricately decorated skin below it. He glanced up at Phipps, whose skin beneath the web of spiraling Polynesian lines seemed European, and found he was looking at a man who had somehow turned himself into a member of an entirely new race. There was no looking beneath his surface to see what he might really be, or what he had once been. The spirals—the words and spirals—the disconnected pictures of monsters, owls, spitting cats, and roses crawling down his arms from below his short sleeves, the skulls and mermaids peering over his collar, gray hairs growing out of their eyes, somehow stopped Ellis from seeing him properly, for Phipps had concealed himself in the heart of his own illustration, and was looking out at the world through a confusing veil. And Ellis knew that he himself was the subject of scrutiny, rather as if he were a challenging canvas filled with spaces that the tattooed man longed to color in.

"I've thought of getting a tattoo myself," he heard himself saying cheerfully.

"Can do!" said Phipps. "No sweat!" He held out an arm, pulled up a sleeve, and flexed his muscles. Naked women, wrapped in vines, writhed obediently. "You ever seen that film *Alien*?" asked Phipps. "We can do aliens, even aliens like you, mate. And we use clean needles every time."

"Phipps likes to put his mark on us all," said Harley. "Don't let him near you!"

"But he *does* use clean needles," someone said over Ellis's shoulder, moving on before Ellis had time to turn his head to focus on the speaker.

"I've had a room here for eighteen months," Harley was saying. "Are you looking for somewhere to crash? They've still got a bit of space." Across Harley's shoulder Ellis could see Ursa arguing with a young woman whose frizzy black hair was streaked with violent purple.

"You watch out for Winston," Ursa was saying. "He's a hard man."

"I like them hard," the woman replied, raising her glass in an apparent toast to Winston.

Then, later—but was it really later? . . . the evening fast turning into a series of brief, simultaneous stage scenes—Ellis found himself squatting beside the pile of tables in the dining room and shouting over the background babble to a tall woman with a bony face half veiled by bright red, waving hair. She was sitting cross-legged beside him and shouting back in a warm but curiously hoarse voice. Ellis knew there were walls around him, but every time he looked steadily at either walls or floor or ceiling, the room changed. He knew the familiar city—his mother's car, his home—were out there somewhere on the other side, but at this moment he felt as if he were suspended in another dimension.

"Oh, yes, Monty was quite the guru back then," the woman was saying. "Always being interviewed on TV and National Radio . . . giving his views . . . telling everyone about the Orono Indians. Then, wow! He really messed up his record. Even his own kids slagged him off, besides being rather sarcastic about the Orono Indians, I must say. And, of course, Social Services just *whipped* his foster children away from him. Well, I mean, he'd been caught screwing one of them. Oh, the drama! But a few years later this lot honed in on him again. Leo and Ursa were independent enough by then, and Foxie came as part of the package. I think Social Services decided to turn a blind eye. I mean, Leona and Ursa are just so capable, and anyway, it's against their policy to split up families."

"Shouldn't think social workers would be very happy to see Fox at a party like this," said Ellis, trying to sound worldly. But his ears seemed to be filled with water, and he was hearing his own words from a distance.

"Yes, but she loves it here," the woman said, "and she's doing well at school . . . well, she sounds as if she is. The principal is one of those educational heroines, and the school gets extra funding because of being multiracial. And most of us here—well—we're all right, in spite of everything. I mean, a lot of us are *kind*." As she stretched out her hand for her glass, Ellis saw that her inner wrist was scored with three bluish lines, parallel indentations slightly puckered at the edges. He must have reacted, for she was aware that her scars had been noticed and turned her wrist toward him with a kind of sad, amused defiance. "Of course, none of us are *normal,*" she said. "But then, what's normal? Do you think you're normal, dear?"

Ellis quickly looked away, searching the crowd for Leona yet again. "Isn't it a bit . . . dangerous?" he asked, hearing his voice sound overcareful. He was struggling to separate his words and finish them off properly. "Living here, I mean!"

"Oh, well, you've got to be careful. But Monty's got some heavy backing," said the woman. "There'd be reprisals. Top you up? By the way, my name's Pandora. I work at Kurl-Up & Dye, just around the corner on Moncrieff Street. I mean, I'm the sole proprietor. I spell that s-o-u-l," she added, laughing and looking at him expectantly, but Ellis did not know quite what sort of expression to assume in responding to this declaration. "I do hair," she explained. "I was looking at your hair earlier. You've got wonderful curls. I'm utterly jealous. But you need a really good cut . . . do you know that? Top you up?" she asked again.

Ellis looked down at his glass and found with astonishment that though it had only just been filled, it was already half empty.

"I must have done a Jackie!" he said uncertainly, remembering how Jackie had drunk so indiscriminately earlier in the . . . but the word "evening" suggested time, and time had stopped. And then . . .

Later, when he tried to remember what had happened next, he found himself recalling a time of great happiness—of true lightheartedness. He remembered singing, remembered dancing with Leona, sliding his hand down her back and pulling her against him as they revolved in a tiny space in the crowded kitchen—a space they seemed to have invented for themselves. He remembered thinking, At last! At last! This is real life. It's a genuine, drunken party, with booze just taken for granted. Not a school thing, where people were self-conscious about drink, and getting drunk was something to boast about. Not his parents' civilized evenings, where people discussed wine in the way that Jackie had parodied . . . *"a pinot noir that tastes of peaches, but is somehow floral as well."* But in the Land-of-Smiles, Ellis was surrounded by people both funny and savage. This was an adventure: he was dancing with a beautiful woman. Later, he was to remember very vaguely, Jackie took his car keys from him, staring at him owlishly, and saying, "No way, mate! Just forget it!" Ursa's voice, speaking from a great distance, was suggesting a taxi, while Pandora advised fresh air. Ellis had tried to tell them what a good time he was having, tried to explain that he wanted to live a dangerous life. But he must have forgotten a great deal more than he remembered, because, when he struggled back into true consciousness, he did not know where he was, or even, for a few dazed moments, who he was. He was just someone somewhere, feeling *something* under his cheek and the palms of his hands. Then feet moved slowly past him *out there,* followed almost at once by other, heavier feet clumping by.

Ellis did not open his eyes. It seemed safer to linger in the darkness behind his lids, for his head felt as if it had split from side to side, and he was consumed by seething illness. Mixed in with this was the memory of great happiness, the feeling of having been set free. And, vivid beyond all other memories, the image of–the name came back to him–Leona. Dreams! He must be remembering . . . a dream. No! He *had* danced with Leona. He *had* pulled her close to him. They had circled together as one person, while an endless party milled around them.

Then whatever he was lying on seemed to spin again and realign itself. Ellis understood, at last, that he was on a bed. It was not one he had slept in before, and neither did he recognize the room, or its muddy, green carpet. Light from an uncurtained window fell across his face. So far, so good: His eyes still worked! He looked wildly around the room. Smears on the mirror, dust on the chest of drawers beside him, cobwebs high in every corner! There, through a partly open door, the end of a bath and a yellowing, plastic shower curtain. His right arm was curled protectively over his head, almost as if he had been fearful that blows might fall on him while he slept. He tested his arm cautiously. The fingers of his right hand tightened and found themselves tracing an alien surface—rounded and faintly bristling. At the same time he felt a hand touch his own head. Horror seized him. His exploratory touch was being affectionately returned. He was in bed with a stranger.

But, after all, both hand and head were his own. Ellis sat up sharply. His stomach heaved, and heaved again, as if it were trying to tear itself out of him and set up a separate life in another part of the room. He leaped out of bed, terrified that he was going to be sick all over himself, but standing up only made things worse. Staggering toward the bathroom, he realized he wasn't going to get as far as the toilet, and fell on his knees beside the bathtub, vomiting into it with relief. Even when his stomach was completely empty the violent heaving did not stop. Pain shot from one side of his head to the other. When the violent retching subsided, a regular drum continued to beat between his ears. Ellis took one shuddering breath and then another. Turning on the hot-water faucet and cleaning the bathtub seemed an impossible job, but all the same he did it, moving like a dazed puppet.

And then, quite suddenly, he felt a little better. He might just live, after all. Given time, he might even become human again. Cautiously, he moved toward the bathroom door, locating a light switch where he had expected it to be. Blinking, he looked around the newly bright room and found himself staring into a mirror.

He recognized himself by yesterday's clothes. They were almost the only thing about him that was familiar. For what he saw in the mirror was a scientific experiment, part living man, and part machine. There was his face imposed on an alien head—a head that was set squarely on *his* shoulders, with *his* shirt tumbling beneath it. Yet it wasn't—it couldn't be—*his* head. It was the head of a robot. It was industrial. It was smooth, rounded, symmetrical, and hairless—not a curl in sight. Hesitantly, he touched the bare crown, and felt the touch on his own skin. Somehow, during a single night, Ellis had changed from a school prefect into an automaton, or some kind of skinhead. Within a few hours he had become a true inhabitant of Moncrieff Street.

PART 2

9 A.M. – *SATURDAY*

Ellis–a man transplanted and transformed–
stepped through the door and found himself standing
between two piles of trash bags, and facing a line of
garage doors. To the right and left of him ran other
doors–the same numbered doors he vaguely remembered glimpsing the night before–interspersed with
long windows, veiled for the most part with faded
green curtains. Turning, he studied the door through
which he had just come. The single chrome number
dangled loosely from a screw, and he could not tell, at
first, if he had slept in Number Nine or Number Six.
He looked at the next door along. Number Ten! So he
had slept in Number Nine. This certainty, small
though it was, gave Ellis the feeling that he was taking
control of his life once more. Then a faint breeze ran
caressingly across his newly naked scalp, and his
stubbled skull responded by prickling all over. Ellis

felt himself become, once more, a confused life-form, squeezed through a wormhole in space from some other dimension.

To his right, one of two green doors opened sharply. Suddenly, Leona was advancing toward him, carefully dressed in a navy jacket and a long, straight, blue skirt. Strands of hair, curling like tiny serpents around her face, made a gentle Medusa of her—a Medusa pressed for time, Ellis realized, for she looked at her watch before glancing at the trash bags, the closed doors, and, finally, at Ellis.

"Have you seen Shelley?" she asked him. "I can't find her and I'm running late."

"Shelley?" Ellis replied stupidly, trying to remember names and faces from the night before. At last, Leona seemed to see him properly. She smiled. Her smile was both knowing and mischievous.

"Ellis! How are you feeling this morning?"

"I'm still working that one out!" Ellis said, smiling as well as he could. His voice sounded, in his own ears, at least, thin and insubstantial.

"No Shelley?" she asked. Ellis, still unable to remember who Shelley might be, shook his head, then felt as if he'd been stabbed from left temple to right.

"Just remind me where I am," he begged her as the dagger twisted behind his eyes, shorting out his vision for microseconds of time. "Who's Shelley? And by the way, who am I?" he added, pleased to find himself able to make a joke of his own confusion. Leona laughed.

"You're in the Land-of-Smiles," she said. "Your

name's Ellis Hudson—or that's what Jackie says, but he's not very reliable. And all the stuff that fell out of your jacket pocket is in the top drawer of the unit beside your bed. I put it there so that, if you flopped around in the night, you wouldn't lose it all over again. *And,* by the way," she said, smiling and mimicking him, "your mother said you were quite right not to drive home."

"Thanks," said Ellis huskily, feeling the remains of his smile grow sickly and embarrassed. "Did I call her?"

"No, I did," said Leona. "You were really out of it. But you almost outlasted Jackie, and that's not easy. I think he's got your car keys, if you need them."

"Did you call *his* mother?" asked Ellis.

"Jackie's parents don't worry too much about him these days," Leona replied. "Sorry! Got to find Shelley. But there's perpetual coffee in the kitchen."

Ellis had been dismissed. Leona walked past him and the trash bags, opening doors and peering into rooms as she went. "Shelley!" she called as she retreated. "Shelley! Come on! No hiding!" Ellis wished he could watch her properly . . . but he was somehow set at a different angle to the world through which Leona was moving so confidently.

So he walked carefully to the left-hand green door, pushed it open, and found himself not in the kitchen, but in last night's dining room, staring, yet again, at the complicated spider's nest of piled tables. And there were the three working tables, placed end to end, stretching out in a more or less conventional fashion. Ellis remembered the crowd he had seen sitting around it when he had first followed Leona and Ursa into this room. He remembered the way the kitchen party had flowed out here when the kitchen suddenly seemed too small to hold them. He remembered Pandora with her scarred wrist, and remembered the woman with the purple streak in her hair refusing to be warned about someone called Winston. He remembered Ursa forcing Fox to go to bed, and remembered how the illustrated Phipps had studied him through narrowed eyes. And now he also remembered sitting at that very table hours later, joking, slinging off at Jackie, and talking eloquently, while other, largely anonymous people listened, smiling as if they recognized the truth and wit of what he was saying. Ellis groaned to himself. What they had been recognizing, he now understood, was his great drunkenness.

At the far end of the table Ursa was sitting, a plate in front of her, and a pile of books beside her. From the nearer end of the table Fox looked back over her shoulder, then turned to stare into her globe of crimson glass, smoldering with imprisoned morning light beside her bowl of half-eaten cereal. Then Ursa looked up, and she, too, studied him, staring through her dark-rimmed glasses, and looking unexpectedly alert for someone contemplating Saturday morning breakfast after a Friday night party. She yawned and stretched, pushing her fingers through her brown mane. "Wow!" she said. "You look dreadful."

Ellis knew it must be true, yet . . . Pretend to be cool, he told himself. He was, after all, going to be an actor. Practice pretending!

"I think I look pretty good, really," he said, running a hand over his newly bare skull. It bristled softly under his palm, and he was surprised by how warm and friendly it felt.

"I wasn't talking about your haircut," Ursa said. "That's the best bit of you. Pandora's an artist. She keeps saying so, so it must be true."

"You said you wanted to change your life," Fox cried. "You kept on saying it! And Pandora did a Number One cut around the sides and a Number Two at the top." She dipped her spoon into her breakfast bowl.

"I thought you'd been sent to bed," said Ellis, quickly improvising the voice of a stern, older brother–rather well, he thought, for someone who was an only child.

"I had to get a drink of water," Fox replied in a slightly whining voice. "I had to come out here and get it. I couldn't help hearing you, you were talking so loudly. Shouting!"

"And Pandora didn't take much encouraging," Ursa added. "She's changed her own life a few times, so she was only too keen to help you change yours. So–haircut, great! All you need to do is to improve the face under it."

"Leo's good at improving people," said Fox, giggling.

"Shut up, you!" cried Ursa. "He's got a long way to

go before he needs any help from Leo. Coffee?" she asked Ellis.

"I don't think I . . . " Ellis found he was simultaneously longing for coffee, and revolted by the thought of it. His stomach heaved violently. Taking a breath, he forced it into submission. "Coffee? Okay! Where is it?" he said quickly.

"Behind the counter," said Ursa, pointing. Turning, Ellis saw a long serving counter, behind which lay a series of electric hot plates set in a Formica countertop. Between two of the plates was a huge coffee-making machine.

"It'll be strong," warned Fox. "Drink water first!"

A bottle of milk and a bag of brown sugar sat beside the coffee machine. A column of waxed cardboard cups, one inside the other, hung in a holder on the wall. He pulled the bottom one free. The coffee smelled not only strong but slightly burned. It was as black as pitch. He splashed milk into the cup and shook in sugar from the bag, noting with dismay, as he did so, that his hand was trembling. Act! he reminded himself. Grab every chance! Practice!

"What a night!" he said lightly. "I didn't mean to get so . . . so carried away."

Good timing, he thought. And his voice had sounded as easy and self-mocking as he had intended it to be. The idea of acting was somehow making conversation possible.

"None of us do, mate," said Ursa, smiling. "And I speak as one of the ones who carried you! But you'll be okay by tomorrow. Tomorrow *afternoon,* that is!"

"Jackie carried you," said Fox. "Jackie, Ursa, and Phipps!"

Ellis sat down at the table. The name Phipps reminded him of spirals, and of blue dragons embracing a naked princess.

"I'll thank them next time I see them," he said. He met Ursa's light blue eyes and made a face. "Sorry!"

"You really aren't any trouble, you know," she said. "It's not as if you're going to eat much for breakfast." At the mere mention of food, Ellis's stomach heaved again. He was surprised by its ongoing resentment. "I suppose you do remember who we are?" Ursa added. "The story so far! Leona, Fox, and I are sisters . . . the Lion, the Fox, and the Bear. Our father named us all after storybook beasts. Our birth father, I mean–yesterday's bad news, dead on the page today. Forget him! It's our foster father you need to remember–Monty! You met him last night, and, later, I heard Pandora gossiping about us all, so you probably know more about us than we know ourselves."

"Three sisters in a castle in a forest," chimed in Fox, making a witchy gesture across the glowing glass ball.

"Yeah! A forest of run-down boardinghouses and scruffy apartments," said Ursa. "We have a never-ending social life, even if it is a bit on the rough side. That's why I was really enjoying the Kilmers' party . . . but never mind all that, now."

"Ursie's going to be a lawyer," said Fox, gesturing at the books by Ursa's elbow. "But *I'm* going to tell fortunes."

The door by which Ellis had come into the dining room opened, and Jackie appeared.

"Morning, all!" he cried, beaming around the room. "Another sunrise in paradise!" His voice, which had begun strongly, quavered on the word "paradise."

"For your information," said Ursa, "the sun rises at about six A.M."

"I'm talking about a spiritual sunrise," said Jackie. "They never take place before nine-thirty A.M."

A phone rang somewhere, seeming to scream in terror rather than merely ring. Ellis jumped.

"Grab that, will you?" said Ursa without moving. "It's probably someone for Leo."

The phone shrilled urgently on and on while Ellis looked frantically up and down the table, and across at empty walls. The sound seemed to be coming at him from every direction at once. Jackie, helping himself from the coffee machine, turned and pointed downward, and so at last Ellis found the phone, which was squatting on the floor almost between his feet. A long, gray cord snaked across the room to a phone jack low in the wall beside the door that led, Ellis remembered, to the reception area. Bending down, he imagined the top of his head was going to flop open, and that what was left of his brain would fall, squelching, on top of the phone. Quickly he snatched up the receiver.

"Land-of-Smiles Motel," he said. His voice was so easy and confident that, once again, he felt proud of himself.

Silence—though Ellis, frowning into the phone, believed he could hear the sound of someone listening back at him from the other end of the line. The deliberate silence was almost a noise in itself.

"Land-of-Smiles Motel," he repeated.

The answer, when it came, was muffled. Ellis guessed at once that the person at the other end of the line was speaking between his fingers.

"*Mumble, mumble . . .* Ursa?"

"It's for you," Ellis called to her, waving the receiver enticingly.

"Who is it?" she asked, making a face.

A door opened. Leona drifted in, smiling and frowning at the same time.

"She says, who is it?" Ellis said into the receiver while he stared at Leona. In spite of his hangover he felt a familiar heat flooding through him, and wondered with dismay if he was visibly blushing.

"Tell her it doesn't matter who the fuck it is," said the voice, suddenly sharply distinct. "Get her to the phone right now."

Ellis was startled by the violence that came punching out at him through the black receiver.

"He wants *you!*" Ellis cried to Ursa.

"Tell him to leave a number and I'll call him back when I'm ready," Ursa replied casually, for she was not the one taking the impact of that unpleasant voice.

"She says to leave a number," said Ellis apprehensively.

"Does she? Well, ask her if she wants to know where the *kid* is," the voice went on, giving the word "kid" a vicious emphasis. "And tell her that if she takes a step–*one single step*–toward the cops, it'll be bye-bye baby."

"What?" exclaimed Ellis, unable to believe what he was being told.

"You heard!" the voice declared. "Think about it! I'll call back." There was a click, and the line died.

"She's just–disappeared," Leona was saying, sounding troubled.

Ursa sighed and got to her feet. "I'll give you a hand," she said.

"Listen . . . ," said Ellis, but too quietly and reasonably to catch their attention.

"I've already looked everywhere," exclaimed Leona, entirely ignoring him. "I've gone through all the rooms."

"The guy who just called . . . ," Ellis began again, but they still talked insistently over him.

"Come on, Foxie," Ursa said. "Baby search! Unless you can tell us where she is from a bit of crystal gazing."

Fox peered into her glass ball. It reflected back at her, spreading an uneven blush across her forehead.

"Hey!" Ellis shouted. "Listen, won't you?" Amazingly, this barking voice had an effect. The three sisters turned obediently toward him. "Someone on the phone . . . ," Ellis began, projecting his voice so effectively that it echoed back from the piled tables. "Whoever it was on the phone said to *ask* you," Ellis went on, using a quieter voice now, "if you knew where the kid was."

Jackie's mouth, which was open as it prepared itself for the first shock of burned, black coffee, closed abruptly. He lowered the cup without taking his eyes from Ellis. Fox turned toward her glowing glass, as if a certain lucky gaze might dissolve its surface and allow her to dive into its hot heart. Ursa and Leona spoke together.

"What guy?" demanded Ursa.

"He said *what?*" cried Leona.

"It was some guy who wanted to speak to you, Ursa, and when you wouldn't come to the phone, he told me to ask you if you knew where the kid was. And then he hung up. Oh, and he did say . . ." Ellis paused.

"Get on with it!" shouted Ursa irritably. "We can take it."

"He said," Ellis explained, hearing his own voice tight with apprehension, "that if you got in touch with the police, it would be bye-bye baby."

"The glass has gone dark," intoned Fox, though no one was paying any attention to her.

"Oh, God!" said Jackie, his fierce exclamation reminding Ellis of his own mother's voice when their dog came galloping into the kitchen with muddy paws mere minutes after she had washed the floor.

"Did he sound drunk?" Ursa asked.

"Blurry!" said Ellis. "Not drunk. Sort of disguised."

"Maori?" asked Ursa. "Pakeha?"

"I don't know," said Ellis. "Neither! Just a voice."

"The glass is darker . . . darker . . . darker . . . "

Though the words were still clear in his head, the

voice in which they had been uttered was already fading, and every question seemed to make it harder to recall.

"It has gone totally black," said Fox, her own voice trembling.

"Oh, shut up about that bloody glass," said Ursa. She looked at Jackie. "This isn't something you've set up, is it?"

"Jackie was here all the time," Ellis cried, feeling obliged to protest against this implicit accusation. He was not the only person to defend Jackie.

"You should trust Jackie," Fox told Ursa, speaking severely, "because you're going to marry him. I keep telling you that."

"Kill first! Marry afterward," Ursa replied.

"Wait till you're asked," said Jackie indignantly. "I'm not going to throw myself away on a lawyer. And thanks for your vote of confidence, incidentally. You obviously think I'd hurt a baby. Great!"

"Sorry," mumbled Ursa. "I know you wouldn't, really. It's just that . . . oh, well, sorry! Sorry!"

"This is mad," cried Leona. "David will be here to collect me at any moment, but I can't go to work, can I? Not with Shelley missing."

"I might be violent at times," Jackie went on, ignoring Leona and glaring at Ursa, "but I'm never, ever spiteful."

There was the sound of a distant door opening. Someone had come into the reception room. Ellis found himself filled with superstitious alarm. He imagined a second door opening to reveal something terrible—a skeleton in a police uniform, say, holding the body of a fair-haired child in its arms.

Leona sighed. "That'll be David!" she said. "But I can't go to work. Not until I know Shelley's safe."

"It's Saturday," said Ellis.

"No closed season for Leona's work," said Jackie. "It just keeps on keeping on, doesn't it, Leo? Always new clients, and none of them can wait."

But the door was opening, and in came a shortish, rather jolly-looking man wearing a dark suit and a silver gray tie. His neatness and cleanness, his slightly pudgy softness looked utterly out of place in the Land-of-Smiles dining room. All the same, judging from the confident manner in which he walked in, Ellis realized that he must know this room well.

"Ready?" he asked Leona, smiling.

"Oh, David," she said. "It's awful. I can't!"

"Another crisis?" His voice was gentle and half joking.

"A bad one!" Leona cried. "Not funny! No way funny!" She caught his arm and pulled him toward the door that opened on to the kitchen. "Come out here and I'll tell you."

But she left the door open, so Ellis was able to watch her talking rapidly and waving her hands, becoming more and more agitated as she did so. He thought about the tottering child he had seen the night before and remembered the way Leona's face had dissolved with tenderness as she had swept the child up, cuddling her close.

"Is Shelley Leona's baby?" he asked tentatively.

85

"She's a kid who was dumped on us. Her mother, Mystique, stayed here during the last bit of her pregnancy, and Shelley was born three rooms farther on from where you were last night. But Mystique took off almost at once, and by now Shelley counts as ours. Leona's crazy about her. We all are."

"Get the cops," begged Fox. "Tell them to creep over the back fence and—"

"Cops don't *creep*," said Jackie. "They charge—like wounded bulls."

"You're prejudiced," said Ursa.

Fox looked over at Ellis. "Jackie was busted last year," she said. "He was growing marijuana, and . . ."

But Ellis, still staring through the partly open door, was watching David put his arms around Leona, though, as far as he could tell, the embrace was nothing more than kind and brotherly.

"Someone must have seen something," said Jackie. "I mean, Shelley always gets up with Leona, eats some sort of breakfast mush, and so on. But there are other people around all the time."

"Not on a Saturday morning after a Friday night party," Ursa replied. "You wouldn't know. You're never up until midmorning, anyway."

"Look! Whoever took her has to be someone from inside the Land-of-Smiles," said Jackie. He paused. Ellis could see him running possibilities through his head, as if he were shuffling imaginary cards. "It has to be someone who knows our ways."

"The glass says to ask Jason," announced Fox.

To Ellis's surprise, both Jackie and Ursa straightened, looked at each other, and then at Fox, rather as if she had made a sensible suggestion.

"Could be worth checking out," said Jackie. "Jason's a real know-it-all. And he's suspended from school again, isn't he? I saw him sitting on the cemetery wall last night as we drove in."

"I saw him sneaking past Norah Prendergast," said Ursa, confusing Ellis entirely. She frowned. "He sometimes nips in here and checks our trash bags. I suppose he could have seen someone coming or going. Could be worth running him to ground and asking a few questions."

Leona was coming back into the dining room, David close behind her.

"She's taking time off work," said David. "No great problem today. We're not busy at the moment."

"Alleluia!" said a new voice. "Things must have gone well this weekend for drunk drivers." Ellis, puzzled once more by senseless comment, turned to see Monty standing in the doorway and looking toward David with that expression of gentle malice that seemed most natural to him.

"Well, it's true that people in my line of business reflect cosmic kismet," David replied so smoothly that Ellis felt sure he had said this many times before.

"Monty, Shelley's missing," said Ursa. "It looks as if it's some kind of kidnapping. Jackie and I are going to try to find Jason just in case he saw someone nosing around our place this morning."

87

"Ask Mystique first," suggested Monty. "She was here last night, wasn't she?" He did not sound particularly interested, however.

"But Shelley was here first thing this morning!" cried Leona.

"Mystique was just cadging a free meal because Winston was working late or something," Jackie declared. "No way would she have taken Shelley back. She's crazy about Winston at present, and if she turned up with a little kid, she wouldn't see Winston for broken glass and dust."

"And black eyes," added Fox.

"We'll try the cemetery," Ursa declared. "Jason hangs out there with Jane Bell and that other kid . . . someone-or-other Lockie."

"Catherine Lockie," Fox said.

"Well, I'll come, too. And so will Ellis, won't you, old buddy?" said Jackie, directing a beguiling glance in Ellis's direction.

"Why drag poor Ellis into our mess?" asked Ursa.

"Because if they make a run for it, we'll need a backup team of four," said Jackie. "North, east, south, and–what's that other one."

"Don't joke!" begged Leona.

"I don't mind helping," said Ellis, "but I haven't any idea what we're looking for–besides Shelley, that is–or where we're going."

"I'm coming, too," cried Fox, leaping eagerly to her feet.

"No way! One of us has to answer the phone," said

Ursa. "There might be another message." A look of doubt crossed her face as she spoke. She glanced at Leona. "Leo, you'd better come with us. Jason likes you, and he might remember something for you that he wouldn't remember for Jackie or me."

"Of course, *I'll* be here to hold the fort," said Monty in his strange, self-pitying voice. "I'm not totally incompetent. I could even write down a message if I put my mind to it."

"I'd come, as well . . . ," began David, talking to Ursa rather than to Leona. "The only thing is—"

"David, one glimpse of you stalking in between the gravestones, and those kids would run for miles," said Ursa. "They'd probably take you for a vampire, whereas Leona and I are just bits of local scenery. And *you're* not coming either, Foxy! Okay—so Monty can answer the phone, but we need you to hand him the pen in case he has to write down any messages."

"I thank you for your confidence," said Monty, rolling his eyes heavenward. But David, Ellis thought indignantly, was looking distinctly relieved.

"Well," he began, "I do have work waiting for me . . ." but he did not complete his sentence.

"Let's go *now*!" said Leona, not listening to him.

David turned toward her. "It'll be all right, Leo," he said with such authoritative kindness that Ellis felt sure he must have been practicing that reassuring voice for years.

Jackie sidled up to Ellis. "Don't worry!" he said. "You won't have to think at all."

"Don't think I could," sighed Ellis.

"All we want from you is blind obedience," said Jackie. "Just do what I tell you to do. Can you bring off a running tackle if you have to? Were you in the first fifteen at your school?"

"As a matter of fact, I was," Ellis replied, glad of the chance to show off a little in front of Leona.

"Games are just practice for real life," Jackie declared in a schoolteacherish voice. "Remember that. Now, follow me."

10 A.M. – SATURDAY

Ellis followed Ursa and Fox out to where his mother's car was parked. All around him lay a country of rust and graffitied fences.

At the sight of the car, he began searching his pockets desperately, filled with fear.

"By the way," said Jackie, half turning his head to talk over his shoulder. "I've got your car keys. I took them last night. You were set on driving home."

Ellis nodded with relief, and tried to look humble. Then he saw that the back-door handle had disappeared. There was nothing but a round hole where it had been, a hole that stared back at him like a sad little black eye. Ursa had also noticed it.

"Did you have money in the car?" she asked.

"No," said Ellis wearily, feeling the back pocket of his jeans. His money was safely there. "My mother might have. She had tapes and things in the glove compartment. Hell!"

He ran ahead and tried the back door of the car, which opened all too easily. He could see that someone had gone through the glove compartment, as well as the pockets inside the doors. The floor under the steering wheel was covered with maps, pens, and the car's handbook. On the passenger seat lay one of his mother's scarves, along with a mileage recorder issued by an accounting firm. The car smelled like the inside of a seaside toilet.

"Someone's peed in here," he said incredulously.

"Sorry!" said Ursa, catching up with him. She looked over his shoulder, sniffing and making a face. "Not that I did it, mind you. But, sorry, all the same, because I didn't think about putting your car in a garage. Everyone round here knows Monty's car and they know it won't ever have any money in it. It's away right now, having rust cut out of it, so it's like my computer–if ever I get it back–more trouble than it's worth. Of course, though, it does confer status."

"There's no status about being carless," said Jackie.

"Never mind!" said Ellis, standing back and slamming the door shut. "Let's find out about Shelley." But he could not entirely hide the fact that he was furious . . . furious with the Land-of-Smiles, as well as with Leona and Jackie, who had walked on by as if the car didn't matter. He was furious, too, with Ursa's fatalistic, almost careless attitude. But most of all he was furious with himself for letting this happen to his mother's cherished car.

"None of it makes any sense, you know," Ursa remarked to him as they hurried to overtake Leona and Jackie, stalking ahead of them. "Someone's playing a trick on us. I mean, the man who called . . . he didn't ask for money, did he?" Ellis shook his head. "That's the only thing people round here want. And, like I said, everyone knows we haven't got any."

"Someone stole your computer, though," Ellis reminded her.

"Whoever stole it is in for a big disappointment," said Ursa as they overtook the other two. "Well, at least your car's still *there*," she said, sounding a little subdued. "Nobody's hot-wired it or anything."

"Lucky me!" said Ellis sourly.

Ursa looked sideways at him. Then she patted his shoulder. "Keep on snarling!" she said. "It's the only way."

10:20 A.M. – SATURDAY

"**We'll** go in by the Rutherford Rise entrance," Leona was saying to Jackie as Ursa and Ellis caught up with them.

"Are you sure?" said Jackie, unexpectedly doubtful. "I mean, past events and all that . . . "

"We're not wimps," Ursa declared. "We're more than a match for the past."

Ellis had no idea what they were talking about. "For God's sake," he said. "Forget the past. Let's just find this Jason and see if he's got any idea where Shelley could be."

Leona smiled at him, pleased to hear someone pushing things along. Ellis's heart gave a small jump of pleasure.

Start small, he found himself thinking, without quite knowing what he meant by this. The phrase just skipped through his mind.

"Money?" cried Ursa.

"We won't need money," exclaimed Leona impatiently. "We're going to a cemetery not a supermarket."

"I've got money," said Ellis, putting his hand in the back pocket of his jeans and taking out various bills roughly rolled together.

In spite of the family crisis, Leona, Jackie, and Ursa all came to a standstill and stared at the money in his hand. Then, for the first time, it seemed to Ellis that they looked at him with respect.

"Well, it's there if we need it," he said lightly, and quickly slid it into his pocket again.

"Just hurry!" said Leona sharply.

Jackie and Leona quickened their pace, and Ellis was left walking behind them once more. His head pounded—once . . . twice . . . then settled down to a sullen ache. His stomach gave a small, nudging heave, but Ellis found he was able to ignore it. He felt himself straightening and becoming more his usual self. It was amazing how much difference even a little money could make.

10:30 A.M. — SATURDAY

Coming out of Garden Lane and into Moncrieff Street, they walked in the opposite direction to the flow of cars advancing implacably toward them. Ellis took a deep breath, aware of the smell of rubber, diesel, and exhaust fumes as they approached the line of old shops.

KURL-UP & DYE, said a flamboyant print on a shop window, and, as Ellis was wondering why that particular name seemed vaguely familiar, someone inside scuttled to the door.

"Looking great!" called Pandora, waving as he passed by. "Am I an artist, or am I an artist?"

Ellis smiled weakly. "Great! Thanks!" he called back, waving as he walked on rapidly, lost memories of the night before slowly reasserting themselves. And now they were passing a narrow section filled with weeds, rubbish, and parked cars. Yet this waste-space was no longer a simple sign of inner-city decay. It had been turned into a strange statement of some kind, dominated by three vast, bright ghosts towering above Ellis and smiling out into Moncrieff Street. The blank wall of the building ahead had been whitewashed, and on the white background someone had painted three huge portraits with photographic accuracy—three people Ellis found he knew. One was of Pandora herself, her right hand tucked coquettishly behind her head. Beside her loomed a vast painted version of Phipps, flourishing what looked like needles between his illustrated fingers, while his gray ponytail blew out horizontally in a wind that nobody else could feel. Back-to-back with Phipps was a portrait of Monty, smiling, and at the same time wincing at the continual flow of traffic. Speech balloons hovered above the three disconcertingly recognizable heads. "Let me put my mark on you?" Phipps was suggesting to Pandora. "Hair! Hair!" she was replying, while Monty admonished passers-by on Moncrieff Street, *"Never forget the Orono Indians!"*

Jackie must have sensed Ellis's astonishment, for he looked back at him, then glanced up at the wall. "You were going the wrong way to see it last night," he remarked. "Great, isn't it?"

"Who on earth did it?" asked Ellis, for those pictures must have taken time and talent.

"Bloke called Weasely Morton," said Jackie. "Wesley, really. Art student. He was shacked up in the Land-of-Smiles for a while, which he loved—also for a while.

Anyhow, he thought art should be out and about . . . everyone living with it whenever they walked to the shop to buy bread . . . and he did several of these paintings round about here. But then he gave in to a job offer and moved north. If he paints anything nowadays it probably winds up in a gallery where only qualified art lovers can see it. But our Phippo loves that mural, and every now and then he climbs up a ladder and alters the words in the speech balloons."

Across the road Ellis saw the sign declaring that it was never too late for breakfast. And it seemed to be true, for there were tables on the pavement, and the smell of bacon and sausage drifting across the road.

The line of shops ended in that curious, triangular building thrusting out toward the endlessly advancing traffic, rather like the prow of a ship confronting oncoming waves. Overhead the electric blonde of the Legges NiteClub grinned up Moncrieff Street. In daylight, with no bright current coursing through her, he could see she had three curving calves, three ankles, and three high-heeled shoes hanging at different angles below her right knee, which was crossed over her left one. From its elbow, her right arm sprouted three forearms. At night she would swing that leg and use that arm to beckon passers-by.

And there was Phipps himself, leaning in a doorway to the left of the closed nightclub door, sleeves rolled up to show his illustrated arms.

SEPULCHRE TATTOOS, said a sign, and an arrow pointed up a narrow stair. A brightly painted poster suggested the various designs with which any passer-by could be decorated if he chose–roses, Maori designs, skulls, tigers, and anchors.

"Hi, Phippo!" said Ursa, waving. She did this in a way that reminded Ellis of someone touching wood for luck–just to be on the safe side. The lights changed, and she charged forward again, following Leona and Jackie.

"What's the rush?" called Phipps after them. "Lost something?" Ellis half heard these words as he, too, began to cross the road. There was a mocking note in Phipps's voice that teased his ear, and even made him look back over his shoulder.

Phipps was watching them with something approaching derision. His mouth opened as if to say something else, but the others were already halfway across the road. Anxious not to find himself adrift in this short stretch of city that had suddenly become a world within a world, Ellis set off after them at a steady jog.

10:40 A.M.–SATURDAY

Turning in at elaborate iron gates, wide open and bolted back, they entered the Moncrieff Street cemetery. Flat slabs lay unevenly tilted in the grass like pages of a demolished book, the names and dates made illegible by weather and moss. More elaborate tombstones rose above them–scrolls, columns, and angels' heads bent as if they were trying to read the blurred inscriptions below them. Yet there was something dignified about these gentle obliterations. Some graves were fenced by wooden palings, or by small stone posts linked by chains, and all were set in a lawn, recently–but roughly–mowed. There, in the middle of the city, Ellis found himself unexpectedly breathing in the scent of new hay.

"Norah Prendergast?" suggested Ursa. She was asking a question, but Ellis, though he remembered her mentioning that name earlier in the morning, neither knew the answer, nor, indeed, understood the question.

"Norah!" said Jackie. "Right! You two try Norah, and I'll check out Eudora Anne." Ellis looked around him, the stranger among these disintegrating markers and memorials. Then he set off after the sisters.

Leona and Ursa were making for a grave that must have once been particularly magnificent. Many years ago someone had planted a graceful tree on it, and now that tree, grown huge, had overwhelmed it, stretching far over the pointed uprights of its fence, some of which were sunk deeply into the living wood. One shaggy branch bent east, a second, west.

As Ursa, Leona, and Ellis advanced, the solitude and silence in which they were moving was suddenly shattered. Like hunted prey breaking cover, two girls and a boy suddenly sprang from the long grass growing under the tree, stared toward them, then jumped into the tree itself, scuttling like spindly monkeys along its huge primary branches until they had disappeared into the thick mosaic of leaves. Ellis leaped forward, keeping pace with Ursa, while Leona turned to shout for Jackie. "Over here! Over here!" she called. "Here! Here!" replied multiple voices, echoing back at them in an angel chorus. Ellis, meanwhile, scrambled gingerly over the iron spears of the surrounding fence, still aware, even as he scrambled, of the scent of newly cut grass. He swarmed up the eastward-leaning branch and, as he did so, saw Jackie charging down on them,

101

leapfrogging confidently over the tilted bookmark of a stone.

As Ellis pulled himself toward the boundary of leaves, a foot in a black sneaker kicked fiercely down at him. Flinging up an arm to protect his head, he gripped the sneaker and felt the foot inside it struggling wildly. Ellis clung on grimly, though he believed he was about to fall out of the tree and impale himself on the spikes below. The sneaker, however, came off in his hands, and the foot hastily withdrew beyond the leaves once more. Ellis pushed himself up along the branch, through the leaves, and found himself staring into the startled face of a boy. He was unexpectedly frail and thin, aged about twelve, dark-skinned, and with short, black hair striped down the center with chemical gold . . . more of Pandora's artistry, perhaps.

"It's only us. It's only us!" Ursa was shouting somewhere from the other branch.

"Don't be scared!" Ellis said awkwardly. "We only want to ask you something."

"Don't *you* be scared, man!" cried the boy in a voice that both threatened and trembled.

"We're not out to get you," said Ellis, doing his best to sound like a Moncrieff Street inhabitant.

"No one going to get *me,* man," shouted the boy, edging farther back along the branch.

"Move on up!" yelled a voice from below him. Ellis obligingly climbed one branch higher, making room for Jackie to burst through the leaves at his heels.

"Jason! What a surprise," said Jackie cheerfully. "Why aren't you at school?"

"Why aren't you?" the boy shouted.

"Wake up!" said Jackie. "It's Saturday. Got you there."

Ellis and Jackie, together with Jason, were held by a cage of branches overlapped by a second leafy cage containing Ursa and the two girls, who now shrieked together in an abusive duet.

"Yeah! Yeah! Yeah!" said Ursa impatiently. "Do we look like truant officers, or cops, or anything? We just need to know where Mystique's living at present. Her baby's gone missing. Jason, you get about early, even on a Saturday morning. . . . Have you seen anyone hanging around our place? Or anyone with the baby?"

"Shelley!" cried Leona from farther down the tree, trying to coax Jason into remembering. "You know Shelley. Dark eyes, and really fair hair."

There was silence. Ellis, looking from face to face, saw that everyone else was looking from face to face, too. The two girls seemed to be seeking some sort of permission from each other to speak out. However, the boy was the one who finally spoke.

"Could be Mystique took her back," he suggested cautiously.

"Mystique!" exclaimed Ursa. "No way!"

"Might have!" Jason insisted.

"Mystique was at our place last night and she didn't

once ask about Shelley," said Ursa, sounding sure of herself at first, yet growing a little more doubtful as she went on.

"She might have changed her mind," cried Leona. "Where is Mystique?"

"Winston might've taken her," said one of the girls.

"Winston!" Ursa exclaimed scornfully. "Oh, sure! Winston loves babies, doesn't he?"

"Mystique's taken up with Winston," said the girl, apparently indignant at having her suggestion rejected. "And Winston's got it in for you lot. He told Mick he was going to bring you down. Because of *him*!" She jabbed her finger toward Jackie.

"Me?" cried Jackie, his expression dissolving into childlike innocence. He risked a quick glance in Ursa's direction.

"Mick says you *hassled* Winston," said the other girl. "He said you'd better watch out. He said–"

Jason interrupted her. "No way does Mystique want that kid back, but she might . . . like . . . pass her on to someone else if Winston told her to. Winston says you lot think you own everything around here, and you'd better watch out."

Ursa looked down at Leona, then at Jackie. Everyone ignored Ellis, already knowing he had nothing useful to say.

"Okay! Next question!" said Ursa. "Where does Winston hang out these days?"

"We don't have to tell," said Jason.

"Please!" begged Leona, crouched on the branch at

Ursa's feet. Ellis could see things were changing. The children had begun to feel that they were the people in power.

"I didn't pick it was you that was after us—not straight off," the boy said in a placating tone. "I thought it was some other guys."

"Social workers!" said one of the girls, and they started laughing, glancing at each other.

"Well, you were silly to climb the tree," said Ursa. "Some of those social workers can climb like monkeys. They'd zip up here after you, no trouble at all."

The bigger of the two girls grinned and pointed. "Go along that branch, and you can get into another tree," she said. "No social worker can get me, man."

"Look! Just tell us where we can find Mystique and we'll leave you alone," said Leona. "Come on! Tell us!"

"We already know she does a bit of dealing," said Ursa. "We're not after her because of that."

"Who's the egghead?" asked the boy, staring at Ellis.

"Just a friend," said Jackie. "Come on." He moved farther into the cage of branches and leaves. "We haven't got all day."

"Yeah, but *we* have," said Jason.

"They've crashed in Burton Street," said the older girl, looking past Ursa to Leona.

"What number?" asked Leona.

"What number?" said the younger girl, mimicking her a little warily. "How do we know what number?"

"It's a blue house," said the older girl, her face

lighting up. "High fence, and that!" She stretched her arm up over her head, illustrating just how high the fence might be. "They don't want no one looking in at them, the things they get up to."

"Is it a gang house?" asked Jackie, sounding, Ellis thought, apprehensive.

"No way!" said the boy. "Nothing heavy! Just . . ." He seemed stuck for words and looked sideways at the girls.

"Private," said the older girl. "It's private. Nothing wrong with being private, is there? No law against it?"

"No!" said Ursa. "I'm glad they're private. Okay! Thanks! We'll call in on them."

"Don't let on we was the ones telling you," said the younger girl. "And don't say Mick told us. Just shut up about it, okay?"

"Silent as the grave," said Jackie, giving an eerie laugh. "And that's really silent, right?"

"Yeah, but Winston . . . ," said Jason. He made a comical face and held both hands in front of him, forefingers crossed. "Okay?" he said, glancing at the others, who laughed and nodded.

"Bug Winston, and he'll rip your face off," said the younger girl.

"Got any money?" asked Jason, changing the subject so abruptly that Ellis blinked.

"Oh, come on!" said Ursa. "Do we look as if we have money?"

She vanished backward through the curtain of

leaves. Ellis glanced behind him and saw Jackie retreating, as well.

"Come on," Leona called, her voice floating up from somewhere below. Ellis looked at the three children. Suddenly they seemed desolate, their faces filled, in spite of their toughness, with momentary longing.

"Don't give them anything," Ursa called, apparently able to read his thoughts even though she was on another branch of the tree. But Ellis had already pulled out a five-dollar bill and passed it to Jason, who took it without a word of thanks.

Then Ellis, too, began to retreat, dropping cautiously onto the grave below. For the first time he noted the name on the stone—NORAH PRENDERGAST: 1856-1902—SADLY MISSED.

Somehow, Ellis had expected to find Ursa and Leona already making for home, but they were both standing outside the spiked fence of the grave, curiously fixed like women caught in a spell, staring around them at stones and grass and trees. For the moment, both Ellis and Jackie were excluded.

"Weird, isn't it?" Ursa said to Leona. "Almost homely!"

"Let's go!" said Leona. "Let's go down and climb over the wall into Moncrieff Street. And then we'll check Winston out."

Jackie and Ellis followed the sisters, winding down between the old graves.

"What was all that about?" Ellis muttered to Jackie.

"What was what about?" asked Jackie, muttering back.

"Something was going on," Ellis said.

"There's always something going on for someone," said Jackie, who looked, Ellis thought, unexpectedly pensive—even, perhaps, a little sad.

11:10 A.M. – SATURDAY

They climbed over the low, stone wall into Moncrieff Street and set off for the Land-of-Smiles, Ursa hurrying after her sister but continually glancing over her shoulder at Jackie.

"Have you and Winston really had a go at each other?" she asked at last.

"Words only," Jackie replied in a slightly subdued voice. "I thought it finished on fairly good terms. I mean, he didn't beat me up or anything."

"The thing is," said Ursa, "he could be counting you and me as an item. He could have decided to get at you through us. And if they've grabbed Shelley, there mightn't be much we can do about it. I mean, it's always been . . . well, an informal arrangement, hasn't it?"

"Shelley's mine," cried Leona. "Ours!" she added.

"She only *seems* like ours," said Ursa. "And you know how keen those children's and young people's workers are on the natural right of the birth mother. Oh, well, we'll check them out." She came to a sudden stop. "Oh, shit!" she exclaimed. "No car! Monty's old wreck is off the road."

"We could walk there," began Jackie doubtfully. But then his eyes swiveled toward Ellis. "Salvation!" he cried, pointing. And suddenly all three of them were looking at him with various kinds of supplication.

Without quite knowing it, Ellis found that a definite agenda had been forming in the back of his mind. He had been planning to find a place where he could vomit up the coffee he had recently drunk. He had also planned to drive home. After accepting criticism from his mother over the terrible state of her car (though he might counter her inevitable anger by pointing out his own good judgment in not driving home the night before), he planned to shower, climb into a clean bed, and sleep until late afternoon. Ursa seemed to detect something of these private ambitions flitting over his face.

"You owe us for a room for the night and a cup of coffee," she said. "Plus all that free booze."

"You got it back again. I threw it all up," said Ellis with a slight smile. He felt this comment was worthy of Jackie himself.

"You had the fun of it, though," said Ursa ruthlessly, "and it's not as if we can recycle it."

Ellis felt his stomach twitch and tighten.

"Oh, please," said Leona. "Just hurry!"

"Well, okay, then," said Ellis weakly. "Is it far?"

"Not if you've got wheels," said Ursa. "And then you can flick us away like used socks."

"No, I don't want to do that," began Ellis. "I want to help. I'd better call my mother, though."

"Leave it until later," said Jackie quickly. "She'll talk you out of it."

"My mom's a good sort," said Ellis, looking at Leona, not Jackie or Ursa. He could see that she had been crying as she walked between the gravestones to Moncrieff Street. "Okay," he said wearily. "It won't take long, will it?"

"Not with a car," said Ursa. "Come on, let's go!"

Leona's eyes may have been red-rimmed, but the smile she directed at him was the smile of an angel—a grateful smile promising future blessings.

11:40 A.M. – SATURDAY

Ellis had the strange feeling that he was under observation. As he approached Garden Lane, breathing slowly and deeply, exerting control over his unreliable stomach, the painted figures of Monty, Phipps, and Pandora watched him. Monty would be trying to match him up with the Orono Indians. "Hair! Hair!" Pandora would be saying, admiring her own artistry, while Phipps would be offering, "Let me put my mark on you." Ellis cleared his throat.

"That Phipps," he said, "the tattooist . . ." Then he paused. Something about Phipps was teasing him, but he didn't know quite what he wanted to ask.

"His family have lived round here about forever," Ursa replied. "The Legges NiteClub was once the family home. Phipps lives in part of the building."

"He thinks he still owns the place," said Jackie.

"And he likes to mark people with his tattoos. Brand them, really. Autograph them!"

"Has he autographed you?" asked Ellis.

"I'd show you right now, but it would lead to gossip," said Jackie.

"Turn left," cried Ursa, who was sitting with the stained map spread out on her knees.

And they twisted through a residential maze, found Burton Street, and, finally, slowed down to a crawl at the sight of a high fence made of plywood sheets nailed to heavy uprights. The house beyond the fence was certainly blue.

"This must be the place," Jackie said. "That fence is only plywood. Let's smash right through it, drive straight up the steps and in at the door."

"Why?" asked Ellis. "The gate's open!"

"It's more spectacular!" said Jackie. "And we'd score a few points when it came to surprise."

But Ellis was already driving calmly into a yard–uncared for, and yet practical, too. He parked beside a stack of firewood covered with a sheet of green plastic. Beside it was a long run for animals made of pipes and wire netting.

"You should have blocked the drive," said Jackie, getting out of the car and closing his door very quietly. But there was no way they could hope to take Winston and Mystique by surprise. Suddenly, the yard was filled with furious sound. Two bull terriers burst out of their kennel and began racing up and down the run, barking both threats and warnings. Leona rushed across the yard toward the red front door. She thumped on it with one fist, rattling the handle with the other. Ursa looked at Jackie, shaking her head and making a face.

The sound of Leona's rattling and thumping filled the yard. Although the door remained shut, Ellis somehow knew the house was not empty. He knew that urgent, furtive movement was taking place beyond the red door, could somehow hear, in between the barking and Leona's spasmodic thumping, a rapid, secretive sliding from room to room.

"Open up, Mystique!" Leona was shouting. "I know you're there."

"Shut up!" hissed Ursa, shaking Leona's arm. "Listen!"

Silence, and then a sharp, snapping sound. Ellis thought he might have heard a gunshot.

"Back door!" said Jackie. "Quickly!"

And, without pause or thought, Ellis found himself bolting around the side of the house, running beside Leona, who might need protection at any moment.

"Be careful! Be careful!" Ursa was yelling behind him, but he could not tell which of them she was warning.

The area at the back of the house was dominated by a black car, luridly painted with scarlet and orange flames along both sides. Even at rest, this car seemed to be smoldering. Ellis blinked. He thought he saw the flames actually flicker, but perhaps the flickering was somewhere behind his eyes. Someone—Winston, he guessed—was already seated behind the wheel, and the same young woman he had seen talking to Ursa the night before was sliding something onto the backseat. Ellis glimpsed a tartan rug and saw a tuft of white hair at the top of the bundle.

"Give her back!" yelled Leona. "Give her back, you bastards!"

But the car was already moving. As the young woman ran beside it in a desperate, crablike fashion, Ellis noticed, once more, the purple streak in her black hair and thought that Pandora, as well as Phipps, must enjoy autographing people.

"Watch out," called Jackie, flinging out his arms to block Leona as the car came shooting back toward them. Mystique now leaped into it, slamming the door after her. Leona ducked under Jackie's arm and made a futile grab at the door handle. Ursa screamed, Jackie swore. But Ellis seized Leona and swung her away as the car shot past them, struck the corrugated iron fence that marked the boundary of the drive, then lurched forward, clipping the edge of the building this time. Gears clashed. The car reversed once more, striking the fence for the second time before swinging successfully round the corner of the house and vanishing from sight.

"Quickly!" cried Leona, apparently unaware that Ellis might have saved her from injury, might even have saved her life. And Ellis, having anticipated her response, was already racing for his mother's car, so caught up in the action that, this time, he was ahead of both Jackie and Ursa. Yet he found he was still aware of Leona's smell, a scent both sweet and tangy.

Then they were piling into the car, Leona slamming the front passenger door with desperate fury, Jackie and Ursa, tumbled and tangled in the back, crying out incoherently. Reversing, Ellis swung onto Burton Street, ready to pursue the retreating car that he saw swinging out recklessly around a distant corner. Instructions burst in on him from three different directions, but Ellis was already accelerating into a pursuit that terrified him, even though he was the man in charge.

"Put on your seat belts!" he yelled, the sort of good advice his mother might have given.

"Just keep them in sight!" cried Jackie. "Jesus!" he exclaimed a moment later as Ellis cornered fiercely, flinging everyone in the car violently to the right. Instructions and abuse exploded around him as he swerved and swayed through a garden suburb, struggling desperately to keep Winston's car in his sights.

"Have you actually got a licence?" cried Jackie plaintively.

"Hey, that was a compulsory stop sign!" howled Ursa.

"Don't lose them," shouted Leona.

The painted flames ahead continued their illusory flickering as Winston flung the black car around a corner and into an avenue lined with oak trees.

"Quickly!" commanded Leona, and Ellis, hearing her voice above the other voices, accelerated, horrified by his own rashness and yet, at the same time, thrilled by it. It was as if he had suddenly turned into the hero of a story that he knew by heart.

They struck a ridge running across the road–a speed bump intended to slow the cars of reckless drivers like Ellis–and became briefly airborne before crashing to the road again.

"Oh, my suspension!" moaned Jackie. The burning car ahead of them, encountering a second speed bump, similarly shot into the air before thumping down.

"I can't . . . I just can't . . .," groaned Ellis, but he found he could. For the second time in a minute his mother's car flew and thumped, recovered, and then raced onward. Ellis forced it to round the next corner so quickly that the back wheels slid sideways, and his three companions cried out in alarm yet again.

"Faster," gasped Jackie in a parody of Leona's voice.

"Do you want to drive?" Ellis shouted back. Jackie was momentarily silenced. "Then, shut up!" Ellis cried. He suddenly realized they had reached the point where the city took to the hills, cutting into them and rising in a series of uneven terraces, punctuated by the exploding green of summer trees.

"Give it heaps!" yelled Jackie. "Floor it!"

Ellis shot through the traffic circle and up the first steep slope, well aware as he did so that he should have given way to an oncoming car that blasted at him in strident reproof before vanishing around the foot of the hills.

"You'll kill us all," Ursa was crying, alarmed by this near-collision, but Ellis was stamping down on the accelerator, and the car, as if given the chance it had often longed for, seemed to take a breath and then surge forward, losing a little power only at the top of the rise. Ahead of them their quarry swung out wide, passing a blue Peugeot.

"Don't get trapped behind this guy," hissed Jackie, straining forward in his seat belt. Ellis, resisting the temptation to shut his eyes as he drove, swept out wide around the Peugeot, even though a blind corner was rushing toward them.

Ursa cried out in protest, "Stop it. For God's sake, stop it!" as they curved into the corner, halfway, at least, across the white line. Then she clapped her hands over her face.

But their luck was in. They were the only car rounding that particular corner at that particular moment. The road tilted upward yet again, but there were no immediate corners to cope with.

"Now!" said Jackie. Ellis felt light-headed—even crazy—but he could not tell if he was crazy with fear and excitement, or because his hangover had suddenly taken charge of him, or because of the bombardment of instructions coming from behind him.

"How about no hands?" he cried, taking both hands off the wheel and waggling them in the air.

"Oh, shit!" exclaimed Jackie, making an impulsive movement, a symbolic half grab at the wheel, across Ellis's shoulder. Ursa dragged him back. Ellis felt an immediate relaxation that was partly triumph. He had successfully terrified Jackie Cattle.

And by now he was part of an unreeling story in which he must act, but over which he had no power at all. The burning car navigated a series of gentle S-bends, and climbed the last, steep stretch to the hilltop where they would find, Ellis already knew, a parking area, and a shop selling postcards and ice cream to tourists. After that, the road would plunge down through a series of hairpin bends toward the sea. But the burning car, its painted flames seeming to blink and shiver, turned left and away from the main road, vanishing between banks of fern and overhanging trees. SCENIC DRIVE, said a yellow road sign, and Ellis also turned left.

In spite of Ellis's reckless efforts, the distance between the two cars was stretching out. Up they went and then down, and saw the other car approaching the first of a series of lookout points. A little beyond, trees closed around the road once more. RESERVE, said a laconic notice, and beside it a second sign held up not a warning, but a symbol indicating the approach of a dangerous bend.

A huge shape suddenly lumbered out of the trees. At first glance Ellis thought some science fiction war machine was charging toward them, but it was an old bus that had been turned into a house on wheels . . . an eccentric compression of engine and architecture. It was more than a caravan. WIDE LOAD, warned a notice attached to the front fender, rather unnecessarily, for the windowed sides swelled outward so that it seemed the vehicle must topple on its wheelbase, crushing anyone who happened to be passing. It rushed toward them not so much straddling, as devouring, the white line, swallowing it up and, almost at once, excreting it. And it managed to do something that no vehicle so far had done. It intimidated Winston, who chose to skid sideways onto the turning zone beside the lookout point, making way for this monstrous, and probably illegal, vehicle to lumber by. The burning car then attempted to spin around and regain the road, but in the act of turning it skidded sideways toward a fence, beyond which there was nothing but space, a hovering hawk, and a view of the city stretching out in the weekend sun. Ellis, horrified, believed Winston's car would smash right through the fence and tumble away, flashing, spinning, diminishing, to crash at the foot of the hill.

Now he himself was also sweeping toward the lookout point. As he drew into the side of the road, the shadow of the monstrous van eclipsed them briefly, but Ellis was watching the burning car strike the wooden fence a glancing blow, then tilt and roar desperately, but to no avail. It was trapped, its left-hand back wheel stuck in some sort of ditch, and it could not free itself.

"Yes!" shouted Jackie, thumping Ellis's shoulder as if Ellis had actually arranged this advantageous disaster.

But there was no time for Ellis to relax and enjoy his triumph. He braked, turned into the parking zone, and drew to a sliding stop, remembering to park in the exit so that even if Winston succeeded in powering his car out of the ditch, he would not be able to escape back to the road.

There were no congratulations forthcoming for this maneuver, which had surprised Ellis himself with its apparent skill. When he took his hands from the wheel, he found he was shaking as if in the grip of a powerful fever, but Leona was already flinging her door open. "Please! Please!" she was saying aloud, but only to the air, and though the car had not quite stopped, she leaped out, staggering forward in a series of uncoordinated, loping steps before stumbling and falling—first to her knees and then full-length. She was up again, almost at once. Winston, a man with tawny, felted dreadlocks, had swung his own door wide and was confronting them, crouching like a mockery of a lion about to spring. Then Jackie was out and sprinting across the turning space with all the enthusiasm of a man longing for action. Ellis, about to follow him, felt the car trickle slowly forward as if it were haunted by a faint ghost of its previous purpose. He had forgotten to put on the hand brake. Spinning back behind the wheel, he wrenched the brake up. And then, at last, he was out, trying to find a place for himself in the confusion around him.

Leona had flung the back door of the burning car wide open and was kneeling, half in, half out, of the backseat. As Ellis registered this, she let out a terrible wail—a wail, Ellis supposed, of grief.

"Oh, no," she was crying. "Oh, no! No! No! No! No!" Five "no's" like five blows.

Filled with fear of what he might be about to see, Ellis reached her side. He was aware that Jackie and

121

Winston were rolling over and over in the dust, lashing out at each other, though with what effect he could not tell. He was aware that Mystique, the young woman with the purple streak in her dark hair, was leaning across the hood of the burning car, shouting abuse at them, and that Ursa, unable to see past Leo, was trying to get a better view into the back of the car by scrambling into the driver's empty seat. But all Ellis could think of was Leona's wailing grief. So he touched her shoulder gently and peered with dread past her bright, tangled hair.

Incongruously, Ursa began to laugh, though it was not a happy sound, while Leona slowly fell to her knees, allowing Ellis, at last, an unimpeded view. What he saw was not a child but a small, gray computer screen, and the square box of the computer itself, wrapped in a yellowish white baby's shawl, full of holes and fringed with creamy wool, and then wrapped again, for concealment and perhaps protection, in a red tartan rug. And Ellis realized that the mad race through town and up into the hills had been for nothing. It had all been a misunderstanding.

12:40 P.M.—SATURDAY

Driving smoothly now, Ellis left the hills and headed in the direction of the city center, where they were embraced again by familiar vistas—houses, gardens, and the wink of traffic lights. But though Ellis was driving slowly, his progress was not altogether safe, for Leona had locked her fingers around his, leaving him only one hand with which to control the steering wheel.

"I really did think it was Shelley," Leona said for the third time, leaning back in the seat beside him, eyes closed. "When I saw that fair hair . . . well, it looked like fair hair, didn't it—"

"At least we got the computer back," interrupted Jackie, lisping because his upper lip was badly swollen.

"I never once thought of Winston—not as far as stealing my computer was concerned," Ursa remarked with a sigh. "To tell you the truth, I did wonder about

123

Prince. I thought he might be someone who'd sell us out if he got a good offer." She looked at Jackie. "Is your lip hurting?"

"Sensitive of you to ask," Jackie replied. "Actually, I'm in agony. But, hey! I took him on, didn't I? Winston, I mean. I thought he'd kill me, but I didn't hesitate. And neither did Ellis," he added.

"Ellis, I'm sorry we all yelled at you back there," said Ursa. "I mean, you drove like an idiot, but I suppose you were doing your best."

"We were bloody lucky, though," said Jackie. "You broke every rule in the book. Wow! Who'd have thought it—a nice boy like you?"

Leona's fingers tightened a little on Ellis's.

"I know I drove badly," he said.

"Dangerously!" said Jackie. "Get it right. You drove dangerously."

"And it was all for nothing," said Leona in a tranquil voice, though Ellis could see she was weeping silently as she spoke. "We still don't know where Shelley is, and she'll be so frightened. And Mystique didn't even care."

Ellis had been stunned by the way the whole confrontation had lost its energy once Winston and Mystique realized they were not going to be called to account for computer theft. Winston and Jackie had immediately moved into a state of truculent neutrality, and Ursa, without further argument, had even been allowed to take back her computer.

"It's junk, anyway," Winston had said.

And at last, circling through the city, they returned to Moncrieff Street, drawing up almost exactly where they had started from, in front of the Land-of-Smiles. As Ellis checked the hand brake, a dark shape danced out into the sunlight, waving both arms, then bounded across to them.

"He's phoned!" Fox was calling breathlessly as she ran. "Called twice. Did you find her?"

"What did he say?" asked Leona urgently.

"Nothing," said Fox. "I answered once, and Monty answered once, and both times, whoever it was hung up without saying anything. It must have been *him,* though, because–"

But before she could finish her tale, they all heard the phone in the lobby give two shrill cries, pause, and then cry again and again. Leona, in the act of opening her door, pulled her fingers away from Ellis's and took off, leaping toward the Land-of-Smiles.

"Leo!" called Ursa despairingly. "Wait! Let me!" Then she ran, too, with Fox at her heels. But Leona reached the front door well ahead of her sisters. Jackie looked at Ellis and rolled his eyes. The phone fell silent.

"Might be nothing," said Jackie, but not as if he believed it. "I'll jump every time I hear the phone for the rest of my life." They walked, side by side, to the front door of the Land-of-Smiles and found Leona in the act of putting the receiver down.

"Was it him?" asked Ursa.

"What did he say?" cried Fox.

"He just said, 'Welcome home!'" said Leona in her

new, eerily tranquil voice. "It was all he would say. He said it about three times."

"Leo, darling Leo," said Ursa. "Don't panic. That's what he wants, whoever he is. And listen! I think we'll just have to get the police."

Leona's eyes flew wide open. "No!" she cried. "He said, 'Welcome home!' He knew we'd just driven in. Don't you see? He's watching us from somewhere close." She spun around staring wildly, as if any of the watching windows that circled the Land-of-Smiles might hide an enemy. "If he saw a police car arrive . . . "

Ellis heard the breath rip in Leona's throat.

"No police!" she screamed at them. Then she turned and, suddenly ungainly, stumbled around the counter to disappear into the dining room. Ursa followed her, while Ellis, watching them, believed he could still feel Leona's fingers twist against his palm even though she was no longer holding his hand. He stared at the door closing behind her.

"Uh-oh!" said Fox. Ellis found she was looking at him as if he were a man of crystal, trouble visibly seething in his heart. "You've got that look."

"What look?" asked Ellis absently. But she merely shook her head, which wouldn't have worried him except that, glancing over at Jackie, he saw in his expression something of the same apprehension that he had just heard in Fox's voice.

"Hey, Foxie, just run and check on Leona, and then report back," said Jackie casually. Ellis expected her to argue, but she moved off without a word.

"You know, you could cut off home," Jackie said. His usual tough-clown expression had changed into something softer and, possibly, sadder. "You need a break."

"So do you," said Ellis.

"Yes, but you're worse than me. I don't think you've had anything like the practice at scruffy living that I've had."

While parking the car in front of the Land-of-Smiles once again, Ellis had certainly thought rather longingly of home, and had planned, once again, to call his mother and reassure her. However, Jackie's suggestion that he might actually like to go home felt like an abrupt dismissal. Defiance freshened him up. He stared back at Jackie without saying anything. Jackie looked him up and down as if he were reading a page.

"Okay, but you be careful, that's all," he said.

"Careful of what?" asked Ellis. To his fury he felt himself blushing for the second time that day.

"Look," said Jackie, "everyone in this house is a bit of a deadbeat. No! Scratch that!" He waved his hands, apparently erasing something written in the air before him. "Everyone in this house is a bit—not mad, not bad—*damaged*. We're like that computer of Ursa's—which I notice she's left in your car, simply asking to have it stolen all over again. We do a few funny things, but they're not—I mean, *we're* not—just"—overtaken by a rare confusion, Jackie stared into space as he groped for the right word—"picturesque," he said at last. "And it's not really anyone's fault, either. It's the fault of the world."

"What are you going on about?" asked Ellis wearily.

"I'm not too sure," said Jackie. "I feel a bit responsible for you, I suppose. Oh, God!" he groaned. "It's happening. I've done my best, but it's happening."

"What's happening?" cried Ellis

"I'm becoming *mature!*" exclaimed Jackie with loathing.

"If it's so crazy, why do you hang around here?" asked Ellis, and as he said this, it occurred to him that Jackie might want to keep Leona and Ursa for himself.

"Good question," said Jackie. "Well, I'm not totally at ease with the world. My family dumped on me—well, half dumped on me—when I was a kid and then, later, I dumped on them—" he broke off. "It's all so *boring!*" he cried. "I'll tell you sometime when we've got a whole day to spare and I can run on and on, making excuses for everyone. Anyhow, by now I'm at home here. And, also, I've got a bit of a thing going for Ursa," he added carelessly.

"Ursa!" exclaimed Ellis doubtfully. Though he had already guessed this, he found it hard to believe that anyone could choose Ursa when Leona was around.

"You surprised?" asked Jackie. "Take it from me, she's ten times as sexy as Leona. Of course, we drive each other up the wall. Oh, God!" he cried again. "I set out to exploit you, and now here I am, trying to look after you. Talk about revenge!"

"You are beginning to sound like a school counselor," said Ellis rather meanly, and Jackie let out a howl.

"I'd never sink as low as that!" he cried.

"What do you think they ought to do?" asked Ellis quickly, hoping to change the subject. "About Shelley, I mean."

"They should go to the cops!" declared Jackie without hesitation. "Just like I think in—" He broke off. "What's that thing you think in?"

"Dunno!" said Ellis, lost yet again.

Jackie's face brightened. "Retrospect!" he exclaimed. "I think, in retrospect, we should have phoned them at once, and that you should have kept to the lawful side of the road during our big chase, and so on and so forth. But there you are. I was screaming at you to go faster, and you were already doing just that. Which brings me back to Leo." He took a breath.

"Ages ago something happened to Leo and Ursa *and* to Fox . . . and they'll never get over it. They've sort of grown around it, but it's part of them forever. And it makes them risky. No! Wipe that! Not so much risky, more unpredictable, but unpredictable is a bit dangerous, isn't it? Look, it's not my story, but maybe I'd better tell you . . . ."

At that moment the door to the dining room opened, and Monty came toward them holding the big glass carafe that usually sat on the coffee machine. "I've cleaned out those disgusting dregs," he said. "We'll start all over again, shall we? Anyone want coffee?"

129

"Both of us do," declared Jackie.

"The thing is," said Monty, "we're out of coffee, and I haven't got any money, and it's Saturday."

"Are you asking me?" cried Jackie, and Monty smiled, shaking his head.

"Oh, no! I'd never make a mistake like that," he said simply, and looked at Ellis, who took the money from his pocket and passed a ten-dollar bill across to Monty, who passed it on to Jackie.

"See what I mean?" said Jackie, pushing the money into his own pocket. "You'd better shoot off home before we eat you to the bone."

"I'm too much part of the story now," Ellis replied. "I've got to know how it ends."

"I'll phone and tell you how it ends," offered Jackie. Then he gave a noisy sigh. "But you won't go. I can see you're too hooked. Well, at least I tried."

"I'll be back in a minute," he added, turning to Monty, "and then we'll have that cup of coffee." He left them.

"I'd better finish my cleaning," Monty said. "At least I can be useful in the kitchen. Do excuse me."

It was the first time since stepping out of Room Nine that morning that Ellis had found himself alone. He walked into the bleak dining room and saw Monty vanishing into the kitchen, but he did not follow him. Instead, he slumped down at the table, burying his face in his hands. He wasn't thinking or feeling anything at all, though a streaming jumble of words and images spun through his head, and he let this jumble flow with its own senseless rhythm, without once trying to give it any shape or form.

The phone rang once more. It was amazing how this ordinary sound now had the power to chill him. It rang twice, and then stopped, so Ellis knew that it had been answered somewhere in the Land-of-Smiles. Then he heard Leona's voice murmuring in the reception area. Almost against his will, but unable to help himself, Ellis crossed the room and opened the door.

Leona was standing there, not so much hunched *over* the phone, as wrapped *around* it, folding it into herself as if anything that might be said into it was too deeply personal to be shared.

Ellis could not make out what was being said, but he could certainly hear the sound of a voice crackling and hissing at the other end of the line. And then, faint and far away on the same line, he heard a distant thread of sound, a wail, unmistakably the cry of a child, and Leona began, once again, that silent weeping with which he was already familiar. Ellis took the receiver from her, and words became distinct.

". . . and don't think I won't *know*!" the voice was saying. "I'm watching you all."

"And I know about you, too. We're closing in," said Ellis, the actor, his voice contemptuous and steely. "Bring that baby back, because, face it, it's you yourself you'll be saving."

There was no reply except an indrawn breath followed by a soft, concluding click. Ellis replaced the receiver and looked at Leona.

131

"You sounded as if you meant it," she said in wonder. "But we're not closing in, are we? We haven't any idea."

Her nose had begun to run a little, and she rubbed the back of her forefinger under her nostrils with a gesture so simple and childish that Ellis, who had no words with which to comfort her, put his arms around her. Leona responded by embracing him with a tumultuous hug, pressing herself against him so hard, it was as if she longed to crush herself out of existence by melting into him. There in the lobby of the Land-of-Smiles they kissed and, for Ellis, Shelley's distant wailing, the horrible phone calls, his mother's damaged car, and his own unfamiliar head—all the concussion of recent events—faded away. There was nothing and no one except Leona, whose soft mouth was sucking just a little at his, as if she had no breath of her own and must steal any he had to offer.

But then, at last, she gave a small sigh, and their embrace was over. She let her arms fall and tried to step back from him. Ellis would not let her go. Leona leaned away from him, her expression suddenly cautious. Ellis knew he must seize the moment, so he kissed her again, trying to consume her, but feeling increasingly consumed himself. Her mouth moved under his again, which was thrilling until he understood, with dismay, that she was actually laughing.

"I must be mad," she said, when she could. "Nice kiss, though," she added quickly. "Thanks!"

Ellis did not want her to say anything, but simply to press herself against him, sealing herself to him forever. "You're . . . ," he began, "you're wonderful," he ended lamely, knowing this was not going to make her look at him with new passion.

"Ellis, you just don't know me," said Leona, speaking as indulgently as if he were a child who must have something carefully explained to him.

"Oh, yes, I do!" said Ellis, struggling to talk reasonably. "I mean, I haven't known you for long—but I do know you for all that. It's as if I've known you forever."

He spoke in a voice that sounded exactly like his but that really belonged to the secret actor in his head. Yet, somehow, now, when he most desperately needed it, the voice was failing him. With every passing moment Leona's softness and her need of consolation were transforming into distance, and even a little hostility.

"So, remind me about myself, since you know so much," she said, still smiling, though by now her smile was shot through with mockery. "How old am I, for example?"

"Twenty," he said confidently. "More or less!" he added.

"More," she replied, still smiling. "I'm twenty-three."

"It doesn't *matter*," Ellis declared, hiding a little flicker of dismay at finding she was fully six years older than he was.

"And how old are you?" she asked him next.

"Twenty," he replied firmly.

"Oh, no, you're not," she said. "Jackie's twenty, and you were a class or two behind him at school, Ursa says. You have to be younger than Jackie."

"But it doesn't *matter*," Ellis insisted, irritated partly by these irrelevancies, but even more by a certain childishness that he could hear creeping into his actor's voice. "Age doesn't matter. Look! I *know* this!" he cried, trying to make himself sound convincing by speaking more loudly. "I mean, I've had a picture of you–a sort of vision of you–all my life. Well"–to his horror he found himself floundering–"not of *you* exactly, but of the idea of you. . . ." He was saying too much, but he couldn't stop.

"Okay! Okay!" Leona struck in, flinging up her hands, palms outward. "Listen, Ellis! On a day like today, real life just crumbles away. There's only one thing that matters to me–one real, main thing–and that's Shelley. But the fact is, I *don't* know you, and you *don't* know me. And even if you did, you probably wouldn't want to. For example, would you like me if we'd met at my work, say, on an ordinary working day?"

Ellis stared at her. He felt she had not understood a word he had said. He knew he was not understanding her.

"I mean, suppose this was an ordinary day?" she persisted. "What would *you* be doing?" As she spoke, she tried to step back from him, but Ellis clung to her.

134

"When you're not driving crazy friends up over the hills, passing cars on the wrong side of the road, and otherwise helping people whose lives are falling to bits because they've been in bits for years and years–what do you *do*?"

But Ellis did not *do* anything–yet. He could not bring himself to confess this to Leona.

"University," he said quickly. "Until the end of next year," he added. Leona sighed and turned her face away, so he was forced to kiss the skin beside her ear. "I'll look after you," he promised her in a low voice, then added, "Leo, I'll never let you go." It seemed to be the truest thing he could say, yet even as he said it he knew it sounded like a line from a tired old song. He wished he could try again, with a slightly different line.

"University! Great!" Leona replied in a tone Ellis hated, for by now she was sounding like some sort of an aunt. "Me–I've got a proper job," she said, and then added, "Sometimes it frightens people. But I think it's pure and central. I'm an undertaker at Dommett & Christie. If we hadn't lost Shelley, I'd be there right now, working with David Dommett–David, who you met this morning–laying out the dead."

At her words Ellis was abruptly flooded with an inner picture of Simon, lying in his coffin, wearing his favorite clothes, and that final expression. Every cell in his brain seemed to explode with this single image, and his arms did not so much fall to his sides as spring away from Leona.

"See? That didn't hurt," she said, stepping back once, stepping back twice, and then retreating still farther. "It doesn't take long for 'I'll never let you go' to turn into 'I can't bear to touch you,' does it?"

"No! Wait!" stammered Ellis. "It was just the surprise."

"There's truth in surprise," Leona replied.

Ellis found the clichés of masterly rapture had completely deserted him.

"I was working on an old man yesterday," Leona went on reflectively. "Heart attack case. We put him on a stainless steel bench and stripped off the clothes he had died in. There were no rings . . . oh, but there were his glasses. I did inventory them, though they were broken. Then I began to spray the disinfectant. . . ." She sniffed her fingers. "He farted a bit. Did you know that dead people fart?"

Ellis made an inarticulate sound.

"Are you disgusted?" asked Leona. "Do you think that's bad-taste information? But farting's one of the things people do. Babies do. So do people aged seventeen. Death is mysterious, but it's ordinary, too. Ordinary!" Unexpectedly, she took a step toward him, and to his horror he felt himself step back. She might have been the one who had inventoried *Simon's* glasses, he was thinking, before he could stop himself. It might have been Leona's slender fingers, the fingers that had curved so warmly inside his own palm only a short time ago, that had given Simon that enigmatic expression, so tentative, yet so final. And now he understood

136

the odd references to Leona's work that Fox and Jackie had made earlier in the day. "Leo's good at improving people," Fox had cried. Perhaps Leona had improved Simon.

"Every day," she went on, "I disinfect dead people, drain the purges—that's what we call fluid that seeps out of the lungs and stomach. Every day I soak cotton wool in autopsy gel and—"

"Don't go on about it," cried Ellis, imagining Simon being purged and disinfected.

Leona spoke sweetly and coolly. "I used a bit of makeup on the old man. Sometimes the makeup we use has lead in it, but he was beyond being worried by things like that."

"Don't go on!" exclaimed Ellis, still thinking of Simon.

Leona looked at him calmly. "I like my work," she said. "I chose it."

"Yes!" said Ellis feebly. "Yes, I know someone's got to do it." And then, because he couldn't help it, he burst out, "But . . . but *you* don't have to do that stuff, do you? I mean, you, you're so . . ."

"So what?" asked Leona, looking at him attentively, like a teacher listening for a particular word to crop up in answer to a question.

"So beautiful!" muttered Ellis.

It was the wrong word. Leona turned away from him, sighing, and saying impatiently, "Do you think only ugly people should look after the dead?"

"No! No, of course not," Ellis cried, furious with

himself and with her, too, for what felt like trickery. He longed to crush the distance between them out of existence once more, but found he couldn't bear to touch her.

"I do my work day after day," said Leona. "And there, at the end, I try to give people back to themselves . . . to their families, of course, but to themselves first. Right now, all I can think of is Shelley, but, since the subject has come up, I'll tell you this. I think my work is noble work."

And she smiled at him, still looking beautiful, yet so alien that Ellis turned and ran from the Land-of-Smiles, humiliated by a horror he despised himself for feeling, but which was too deep and ancient to be resisted.

1:10 P.M.—SATURDAY

His mother's car, no longer quite the car it had been this time yesterday, was waiting patiently. It had not only been defiled but had been driven in a fashion that would have horrified his mother. Ellis touched its hood with brief compassion before opening the door and scrambling in. As he felt in his pocket for the car keys, he screwed up his face at the smell.

Staring blankly out through the windshield, he found himself meeting, through a narrow slot of space between the buildings in front of him, the hard gaze of Phipps, the painted Phipps. There was something quizzical in the way the painting regarded him, and, out of the blue, Ellis found himself remembering the real Phipps—the one who had spoken to him earlier in the day. He remembered how he had hurried past, anxious not to let Jackie, Leona, and Ursa cross the road without him, and how Phipps, watching him go by, had said . . . what was it he had said, exactly?

Sitting there like a stale and weary shell of himself, Ellis pondered on the knowing and secretive glance he and Phipps had accidentally exchanged, and seemed to be exchanging once again. He recalled, with great distinctness, a certain taunting challenge in Phipps's expression, and suddenly felt certain that his smile had contained some kind of coded message. "Lost something?" That is what Phipps had asked him, but it was not so much the words as the voice in which they had been spoken that now troubled Ellis. For if he could sit there in front of the Land-of-Smiles and see the painted Phipps looking back at him through a narrow gap in intervening walls, might not the real Phipps be able to climb up to some rooftop perch (up above Legges Nite-Club, say) and watch all comings and goings from the Land-of-Smiles?

Why would he, though? Ellis asked himself scornfully. He had had enough . . . he had just had enough! He had partied hard, and overpartied. He had driven a car in a Hollywood kind of car chase. He had fallen in love and been rejected. Death had confounded him not with its terror—he could have accepted terror—but by revealing itself as mundane. He had made many mistakes, and certainly he did not want to make yet another. He'd had enough. More than enough. Why set himself up for more? He would go home immediately.

Shaking his head, Ellis half turned the car key, then paused, frowning down at the fingers still clamped to the key. This time he was sitting in the car on his own. He was not hurrying like a well-trained dog after Jackie, Ursa, and Leona. No one was shouting instructions at him. This time he was free to think for himself, to think as precisely as he could about the mocking way Phipps had asked his simple question, and even more about the expression he had worn, and the way an unstated knowingness had somehow oozed out through the enigmatic blue spirals on cheek and chin. Ellis felt certain that there had been something suggested—intimated—though nothing had been declared.

He thought briefly of his mother once more. By now she would be worried—very worried—at not hearing from him. And what would she say when she saw the door of her car? What would she say when she saw his naked head?

Yet how could he leave the Land-of-Smiles without knowing what had happened to Shelley? How could he tear himself out of the story when he had been in it from the beginning and might even have picked up a clue that nobody else had?

So, at last, Ellis climbed out of the car, locked it once more, dropped the keys in his pocket, and set off wearily, annoyed with himself because, though he couldn't believe his own woolly hunch, he couldn't let it go, either. He jogged down the right-of-way, down Garden Lane, and back into Moncrieff Street, bound for Sepulchre Tattoos.

"It's probably shut," he said aloud to himself as he

jogged. Leona's recent conversation ricocheted around in the back of his head. Not her exact words—he found himself shrinking from remembering her exact words—but something of their energy and impact. He ran past the health shop, past Kurl-Up & Dye, and past the Book Exchange, all locked so tightly, it was as if they were sealed shut. Across the road people were still discovering that it was never too late for breakfast, while others made for the Grenadier Tavern. Ellis felt, with surprise and a slightly sad exhilaration, that these shops (which had once seemed nothing more than stage props) were, nevertheless, a true neighborhood. Indeed, they had somehow become *his* neighborhood.

He paused by the traffic lights outside the door to Legges NiteClub. Almost as if they had arranged to meet at this very moment and on this very spot, Phipps came to the door under the sign that read SEPULCHRE TATTOOS. Their eyes met. Phipps's gaze felt almost like a physical touch as it ran over Ellis's newly bare head.

"Tattooing business slow?" Ellis asked, and was pleased to hear that his secret acting voice had regained its power. Not that he had set out to sound powerful, merely ironic, casual and unimpressed.

"It's been steady," said Phipps. "There's a lull right now. Might be busy later on. People get impulsive after a few drinks. Ever thought of having a tattoo yourself? Something to set off the new hairstyle?"

"I hadn't thought of it," said Ellis, remembering that Phipps liked to put his mark on the residents of the

Moncrieff Street village, but determined he was not going to put his mark on him.

"Saw Monty wandering by a little bit earlier," Phipps said. "Find the kid?"

"No!" said Ellis. "She's still missing. Actually, I thought—I just had an idea from something I remembered earlier—that *you* might have some clue where she might be."

"Dunno about that," said Phipps. Then . . . "Well, maybe! Not a real clue! More of a hunch." Then he fell silent, staring at Ellis as if he was waiting for him to make the next move. Ellis knew that he could get no more information from Phipps unless he made the right move.

"If I came in . . . I mean, how long would it take to have a tattoo done?" he asked, tentatively, at last. Phipps's map of a face seemed to ease into a slightly different configuration. "A little one!" added Ellis quickly.

"Thirty minutes, more or less," said Phipps. "Do you want to see what's available?" He gestured at his door, and then vanished through it.

Ellis followed him. "If you know where she is . . . ," he began.

Phipps shook his head. "I don't!" he said. "No idea!"

"Come on!" Ellis begged. "They're desperate at the Land-of-Smiles."

"I'd have told them if I knew anything," Phipps said. "I'd have *said*."

The room Ellis had entered was lined from floor to ceiling with laminated posters displaying a whole range of small, disjointed pictures, and he felt as if he himself were one of them—a cartoon figure fallen from a disorganized comic strip. These pictures, these fragments of design, these bony hero-faces, these leaping, plunging action-men, were somebody's art.

"Take a good look around!" invited Phipps expansively. Behind the counter a middle-aged woman with long, rippling red hair smiled at him with such amused complicity, it was as if they had agreed to share some joke at the expense of the world. Ellis wished he could be sure just what the joke might happen to be.

There on the wall behind the woman was a sheet displaying Maori *moko,* a traditional tattoo design covering the chin, and similar tattoos. Beside it there was a series of pictures of a whole regiment of comic-book girls, pouting as they tossed long, blond hair and thrust large, rigid breasts toward the observer.

"Are you offering to tell me something useful if I have a tattoo?" he asked bluntly.

"No," said Phipps. "I probably don't know anything useful. But work brings out the old woman in me. I gossip about all sorts of things."

"He does, too," said the redheaded woman, laughing as if Phipps had said something witty.

"Suppose we're halfway through the tattooing and then suddenly I realize you're fooling me," Ellis said.

Phipps shrugged. "Live dangerously!" he suggested.

"You'd have the tattoo, so at least it wouldn't be time wasted. It'll match up with that haircut."

"Be coordinated," said the woman.

Beyond the images of the girls was a chart filled with skulls, some embraced by curling vines, and some imposed on racing cars, or Harley-Davidson motorbikes. Others had lightning bolts shooting out of their hollow eyes, or were wreathed in flowing hair.

"How about one of the girls?" asked Phipps.

"No," said Ellis slowly. "No!" If he took a step toward death, if he joked with it, it might retreat . . . grow circumspect. He might in some way put Simon in his place, be able to grieve for him in a simple fashion, without feeling that he had somehow been faced with a challenge he could not meet. "I'll have a little skull– one with a sense of humor."

He pointed at one with a rose in its teeth. The rose was crimson, with green leaves. The skull's round eyes were electric blue. It smiled around the rose as if it were making fun of him.

"That one!" said Ellis.

"In here!" said the woman, pointing. "Don't worry! We use new needles every time . . . new ink! We're really good on color work!"

Ellis had not even considered the possibility of infection.

"Some people get big pictures done," the woman ran on. "Sit down here, dear. Mind you, they don't get them done in one go–just as they can afford it. We've got one bloke having his back done . . . a big Crucifix-ion and a view of Jerusalem. Phippo's laid down the outline, and now we're doing the coloring in, bit by bit. It'll cost him about fifteen hundred dollars by the time it's finished."

As she talked, she was settling Ellis in a narrow chair, fitted into a narrow space. Phipps was shuffling through what seemed to be a filing drawer.

"Here it is," he said. "We put a transfer on you first. I won't have to improvise, though I can do so if I need to," he added rather boastfully. "We'll have you fin-ished in next to no time." The woman was swabbing Ellis's arm with disinfectant, which reminded Ellis of what Leona had said about her own work. He pushed her out of his mind.

"Do you know Ursa and Leona well?" he asked rather awkwardly.

"Well enough!" said Phipps. His voice was guarded, but there was satisfaction in it, too—the satis-faction of someone who sees nervous prey working its way toward a cleverly placed bait. He thinks I'm doing what *he* wants, thought Ellis. "I know everyone around here," Phipps continued. "Well, my family's lived here since the year dot. And the Hammonds have been here a good while as well."

"Phipps thinks he's king of the castle," said the woman. "But what I can't work out is why the Ham-monds stay on. I wouldn't, not after what happened, back then."

The needle stung Ellis's arm—a tiny, fretful, persistent stinging . . . *Zzzt! Zzzt! Zzzt!* Like a trained mosquito. "What *did* happen back then?" he asked lightly.

"Thought everyone knew!" cried the woman. "It was famous at the time. The Hammonds lived down by the cemetery when they were kids, the two girls, their brothers, and the little one. She was only a baby, though. Shouldn't think she'd remember much about it."

"Shouldn't think the others could forget," mumbled Phipps, almost to himself.

"Remember what?" asked Ellis. He had not come here to spy out the pasts of Leona, Ursa, and Fox, but he was astonished at how much he suddenly wanted to know everything about them. Besides, he could tell that Phipps was enjoying his moment of power. It was making him expansive. The redheaded woman took a breath, but Phipps got in first.

"Their old man shot their mother," he said. Ellis could see he was irritated by the thought of someone else telling an outsider local gossip.

"He shot his wife, then woke the kids, marched them into the cemetery, and shot the two boys," the woman went on.

"And then . . . and then he shot himself," Phipps added, finishing the horror story. "Family life, eh?"

Ellis remembered the way that Leona and Ursa had stood staring around the cemetery, earlier in the day, and wondered if Phipps had expected to shock him with his casual dismissal of such a terrible story. But Phipps was concentrating on the nimble needles, skipping and stinging across the skin of Ellis's upper right arm.

"I don't think they're worrying about past stuff right now," Ellis said at last. "That little kid they look after is missing."

"Mystique's kid?" said the woman. "Yeah! Monty told us. Perhaps her mother's decided to take her back so she can claim child support."

"When I went past you this morning," Ellis began, "you asked if we were looking for anything. . . . You sounded as if you might know something you weren't telling."

"Phippo!" exclaimed the woman. Suddenly, she seemed a little threatening. "Were you playing one of your games?"

"I didn't know the kid was missing then," said Phipps defensively. "It's not like anyone told me anything. You all just marched by, looking jittery. And then I remembered seeing something this morning. Mightn't mean anything, but you never know."

"Oh, Phippo!" said the woman, rolling her eyes. "Didn't you say anything to Monty when he looked in?"

"There wasn't anything to *tell*, not anything much," said Phipps, sounding harassed. "Anyhow, sometimes those Hammonds act as if they own Moncrieff Street, and it gets up my nose."

"What did you see?" asked Ellis.

Phipps regained his composure and grinned at the needle tingling across Ellis's skin.

"Phippo!" repeated the woman sternly.

"Okay! Okay!" exclaimed Phipps. "I was out and about early this morning, like always, having breakfast over at the café, like always–"

"Bacon and eggs and sausage," the woman cried, interrupting him. "He'll kill himself, won't he? All that cholesterol!"

"And–*and*–I saw a particular car–a car I knew–turning into Garden Lane."

The needle stung, but it was a lot less uncomfortable and painful than having a tooth drilled.

"This car–you can't help recognizing it–expensive red job. It belongs to that kid who comes slumming around here with everything hanging out–tongue, dick, everything. Anyone can tell he's really hot for her, and he's one of those kids who has had the lot and doesn't see why he shouldn't have a little bit more," said Phipps. There was certainly irony in his gaze as it lingered on Ellis.

"Who is this character?" Ellis asked suspiciously, but Phipps was enjoying his moment of revelation and wanted to spin it out.

"Listen," he said. "I'm telling you, aren't I? I saw his car. And then, just a few minutes later, I saw it pulling out again. So it wasn't a social call. Must have been about nine A.M. And he took off down the road like a bat out of hell . . . ran a traffic light . . . vanished!

You probably know the guy. Longish fair hair, and a beauty spot, right here."

And Phipps's finger reached out like the finger of a witch in a Disney cartoon to touch a point on Ellis's cheekbone. As his eyes met Ellis's in the mirror, he kissed the air mockingly, then laughed.

"Christo Kilmer!" cried Ellis. He had intended the name to be a question but, almost simultaneously, he knew the answer—knew it for sure. He thought of the toddling child. He thought of drowning kittens. All day he had been anxious, but his anxiety had been a reflection of other people's distress. Now he felt a true horror that was all his own.

"Christo?" said Phipps, tasting the name. "Christo! Could be. Fact is, we've never been introduced. I've just seen him around. And I've listened to gossip."

"Why didn't you tell them?" asked Ellis. "Ursie and Leona, I mean! Or Monty!" He glanced sideways at the needle stinging his shoulder. He could see something like a knot of dark color developing there, with a pink blush extending on either side.

"Well, what do I know for sure?" said Phipps, shrugging. "I mean, half the weirdos in the district drop in for coffee and God knows what else at the Land-of-Smiles . . . and that Monty—he still thinks, deep down, that he understands people, whereas most of them are just ripping him off, the poor old has-been. As for the Hammond girls . . . well, we've touched on their particular family circumstances, haven't we? Gives a new meaning to nuclear family, I reckon."

Ellis was, at that moment, so swollen with possibility that he felt he was about to explode. Christo! Christo Kilmer! They should have known–*he* should have known. He should have known immediately! He should have recognized that voice on the other end of the line. Think! Think! he commanded himself, trying desperately to bring to mind anything about Christo that might give further clues. Christo's parents were separating . . . only last night Jackie had stolen Ursa away from him. . . .

"The kid in the red car–Christo, did you say he was?–I reckon he's questionable," said Phipps suddenly. He winked at Ellis in the mirror. "Takes one to know one," he added, "and I've met a few. That kind turns nasty when they don't get what they want . . . and he's not going to get Ursie, is he? She's too sharp for him."

The words Phipps spoke dropped into Ellis's head like smooth, oval stones, falling, almost soundlessly, into a deep dark pool. The pool accepted them silently. What Phipps said felt true.

"Okay–that's you done, mate, and looking good!" said Phipps, admiring his own work.

Ellis stared down over the curve of his shoulder, but he could not see much. A moment later Phipps had folded a piece of gauze and was strapping it over the tattoo with tape.

"Now, it'll probably scab a bit," he told Ellis. "But

the scab just flakes away. Put a bit of antiseptic cream on it if you like, but it should be fine. Never had any complaints, anyway."

Ellis got to his feet. All he wanted to do was to run back to the Land-of-Smiles.

"I reckon I've made my mark on you," Phipps commented with satisfaction. "That'll be forty dollars."

Ellis looked back at him and, as he did so, felt a new, unanticipated power flood through him. "Actually," he said, "it's not your mark, it's mine. Firstly, I chose it, and secondly, I'm stealing it. Because I'm not going to pay you."

Phipps's smile vanished.

"I've got the money," Ellis went on, "but I think you owe us something because you didn't say a word about any red car."

"I could be making a mistake," said Phipps dryly. "I sometimes do." The corners of his mouth turned down in private discontent, but he seemed to accept that Ellis was the true representative of the Hammond sisters. "It is my mark," he declared. "Come on! Pay up, or there'll be trouble."

"It's mine now!" said Ellis. "Mine forever!"

Then, turning his back on Phipps, he dived for the door, taking both Phipps and the redheaded woman by surprise, and leaped out into Moncrieff Street, running with an energy, almost a lightheartedness, that surprised him. He was running back to the Land-of-Smiles, his tattoo burning a little on his upper arm, and his head unexpectedly cool in the afternoon breeze.

In spite of his lingering hangover, in spite of feeling so battered and bald, in spite of his fears for lost Shelley—stolen away, he was sure, by Christo Kilmer—Ellis laughed a little as he ran, gathering his new power into himself and hoarding it there like treasure.

3:10 P.M.—SATURDAY

When he burst through the dining room and then into the kitchen, a television set was playing. Frenetic cartoon figures jived across the screen, shouting and gesticulating. Monty and Fox were watching these together, Monty looking as if he had not moved from his big chair since the night before.

"I know where she is," yelled Ellis. "At least, I'm pretty sure I do."

"Back so soon?" said Ursa. He hadn't seen her at first, half hidden by the open door. "I thought you'd gone for good."

"I told you he'd be back," said Fox complacently, tapping the bubble of glass a little to her left. "Glass tells all."

Ellis ignored her. "Christo! Christo's got her," he cried. "Shelley, I mean. I had a thought, and I asked

154

Phipps, and he said he'd seen Christo's car coming out of Garden Lane at about nine this morning."

"Oh, God!" exclaimed Ursa. All day she had greeted various crises by looking alert, or looking alarmed, or looking angry. But now, for the first time, she looked stricken. "Christo!" she said in a soft voice. "I never once thought of him. Why didn't I?"

"Christo!" exclaimed Leona, appearing through the doorway that led to the trash bags. "Did you say *Christo*?"

"Ellis thinks he's the one who's taken Shelley," Ursa said. The words came out stiffly as though they were unwilling to be spoken.

"Christo?" cried Leona. "Why would he?"

"He's a bit crazy," Ursa said. "And I did sort of walk out on him last night."

"Christo!" exclaimed Jackie's voice, and Jackie himself loomed up behind Leona, his voice a darker echo of hers. His right eye had blackened and swelled. He looked out at them through a sinister, gleaming slit, his upper lip drooping grotesquely over his lower one. He put out his hand, stretching past Leona toward Ursa.

"Sorry!" he cried with real fear and pain in his voice. "Sorry! Sorry! It's my fault. I should have left you alone. Sorry!" He looked at Ellis. "Where is he? I mean, he must be somewhere close, because he knew when we came back from chasing Winston over the hills."

"Is he keeping her in his car?" asked Leona. Ellis knew she was imagining the baby gagged, tied, and perhaps stuffed in a box or suitcase, locked up tightly and struggling to breathe. He was imagining it himself, imagining it with such close sympathy that his breath caught in his throat. Out of old memories, Christo's bare foot, the toes feeling so competent—almost pre-hensile—came down on his head to push him once more under the muddy water of the old swimming hole.

"The Kilmers have an apartment in the old library complex," he said. "You know, on Foley Street." He pointed in the direction of the city center.

"Could he see us from there?" cried Jackie.

Ellis shrugged. "It's more or less in a straight line from here," he said. "With binoculars, say? Maybe!"

"Then let's check it out. Now!" yelled Jackie. He and the two sisters spun toward the door, then hesitated. All three of them turned and looked back at Ellis, Leona perhaps a little unwillingly. However, there was no choice. She had to appeal to him, because he was the man with the car.

"Let's go!" Ellis agreed, and felt for his car keys, a little like the good sheriff in a Western feeling for his gun. They charged ahead and he followed, leaving the Land-of-Smiles for the fourth time that day. But this time, at least, he was in charge. He may have been following the other three, but, whether they knew it or not, Ellis was the leader.

PART 3

4 P.M.—SATURDAY

Time was bending back on itself. Nearly twenty-four hours earlier, Ellis had walked up the road along which he was now driving. He wondered how he could be so sure that he was still last night's man, yet, at the same time, feel certain that he had completely altered. Lights changed, and without needing a single shouted instruction, Ellis turned right onto Foley Street, which now struck him as unnaturally clean and artificial. The elegant, spindly signs, the streetlights sporting red hoods on long, green stems, looked like pieces in an expensive game being played on behalf of people who could afford to play. And there, in front of them, was the old public library, transformed and still transforming. It looked like some grotesque insect bursting out of a cocoon. The cage of orange-colored scaffolding clamped it in as if it might possibly turn dangerous—as if it might need to be restrained. Ellis drove toward it, one in a line of cars, all probably searching for parking places.

SECOND STAGE DEVELOPMENT, said a notice.

There was no visitor-parking area. Indeed, there were dire warnings on the small, paved area in front of the building that illegally parked cars would be wheel-clamped or taken away. On the far right a line of blue-doored garages vanished behind the building.

"Shall I risk it?" asked Ellis without needing to say what he was talking about.

"Better not!" said Ursa. "Suppose there's no one at home and we come back to find the car gone?"

"Suppose we need to get away quickly?" added Leona.

"We might have another car chase," Jackie said, making a ferocious sound that suggested desperate braking and cornering.

"Don't joke!" yelled Leona, but Ellis could not tell if it was grief, terror, or fatigue that was roughening her voice.

"I have to," Jackie cried back. "I can't help it. You ought to know that by now."

"There!" cried Ursa, pointing.

Only a few spaces ahead of them a car was sliding carefully out of a parking place.

"Oh, for Christ's sake," exclaimed Jackie, for the car ahead of them was backing greedily toward the vacant space.

But, once again, Ellis amazed himself. He accelerated, and then, angling sharply past a parked green

Mazda, slid into the space with the sort of assured rudeness he had often resented in others. The right-hand side of his mother's car had scraped against some part of the Mazda, but the parking place was definitely his. The driver of the rival car, after making a gesture of disgust, changed gears and drove away.

"Right *on!*" said Jackie in surprised admiration. "Hey, who taught you to drive?"

"My mom," said Ellis, jamming on the hand brake. "I think I took a bit of paint off that Mazda, though."

"At least there was no one sitting in it," said Ursa.

They scrambled out as they spoke–Jackie, Leona, Ursa, and Ellis–and turned toward the old library.

"You stay here," Ellis said to Jackie.

"No way," said Jackie.

"Think about it!" commanded Ellis. "Just suppose Christo is up there somewhere–just suppose that, right now, he's looking out of a window. . . ."

"Ellis is right," said Ursa.

"I'll slide along next to the wall," said Jackie, looking right, looking left, then setting off across the road. "Even if he does look out of the window, he won't see me."

"He might have seen us already," said Ursa gloomily, "if he really has been watching the Land-of-Smiles from somewhere up there."

"That's why I drove in a loop," said Ellis. "He could have seen us setting off, but–"

"Come on!" Leona cried softly. "He can't possibly have seen us. Even if he could see all the way to

Moncrieff Street, he wouldn't be able to tell one person from another."

There was no time for further argument. They skirted the old building, crossed a courtyard, and climbed steps to grand, green main doors, with panels and decorative brass locks. The small, square lobby inside was dominated by an elevator. Along the left-hand wall, numbered mailboxes opened gaping, oblong mouths, while on the right-hand wall, opposite the mailboxes, was a series of small grids, all numbered and named to match the mailboxes.

The name KILMER, gold print on an enameled green plate, stood out beside Number Twelve.

"Here we go!" said Jackie, his finger hovering over a red button with the word COMMUNICATE beside it. But Ursa slapped his hand away.

"My job," she said. "He'll freak out if he gets any idea that you're here. But he'll let *me* in–if he's there, that is."

"Oh, please . . . ," sighed Leona. "Please!"

But Ellis was pressing the button with one hand and gesturing for silence with the other. They waited.

Miraculously, a voice came crisply from between the narrow bars in front of him. . . . "Hello, there!" it said carelessly. And indeed it was Christo. Ursa clapped her hand over Jackie's opening mouth as if unguarded words might slide out of it.

"Christo?" said Ellis in a slightly doubtful voice. "Is that you?"

"Who's that?" asked Christo, too sharply for a man

who had been merely relaxing and watching television.

"John Marlin," said Ellis, snatching a name out of the past. Remembering the voice that had once gone with that name, he deepened his own slightly, careful not to overdo it, and assumed a faint Scottish accent. "Just passing through and thought I'd check up on a few old friends." (Right on, he thought with satisfaction. That's exactly how John used to sound.)

"Hell!" Christo's voice had relaxed once more. "Where did you spring from?"

"I'm en route to Dunedin," said Ellis. (Not quite so convincing that time, he thought.) Christo, however, did not seem at all suspicious. "I called your parents, but they weren't too sure where you were. They gave me this address, though."

"Were they worried?" Christo asked, his voice sharpening once more.

"Worried?" said Ellis in a puzzled voice. "Why would they be worried? Are you up to something?"

"I've got to have *some* private life," said Christo bitterly.

"Well, how about letting me in?" asked Ellis plaintively. "I've got a few cans and a bottle of gin."

"I'm not short of booze," said Christo, deriding this bribe. "This place is always pre-e-tty well stocked."

"Let's party, then," Ellis cried exuberantly. Christo was silent. "Come on!" he repeated desperately. "To tell you the truth, mate, I'm on the run."

"Why? What's happened?" asked Christo, suddenly interested. Ellis was tempted to invent something, but–

no, he told himself sternly—keep it simple.

"Just let me in," he begged. "I can't tell you my life story while I'm standing out here."

There was no reply. Ellis could feel Christo's doubt as if it were a sort of electricity arcing down through the communication system and into the air of the lobby. Jackie was staring at him with flattering astonishment. But then all four of them focused on the intercom, standing a little on either side of it as if an eye might look down through invisible wires and see who was really there.

"The thing is," said Christo at last, "I'm not quite alone. But—okay! Come on up."

"This is all wrong," said Ursa as they crammed themselves into the tiny elevator. "He'll take one look at us and—"

"If he won't give her back, we'll have to call the police," said Leona. "At least we know where he is."

"We don't actually know that he's got her," said Jackie.

"Yeah," Ellis said. "But it's getting more and more likely. Don't you think he sounded . . . a bit funny?"

"Right!" said Jackie with subdued sarcasm. "A real stand-up comedian. But you were great. How do you do that Scottish thing?"

The elevator door opened. They came out into a small area carpeted in dark blue and with two doors opening off it in different directions. The left-hand door displayed the number 12 in shining brass. Ursa, Jackie, and Leona flattened themselves on either side of the door, acting like characters in a television police drama. Ellis faced the door squarely and knocked. The handle rattled and turned. Christo must have been waiting for them. The door opened a reluctant centimeter or two, just enough to let Christo peer out at whoever might be on the other side.

With a yell, Jackie flung himself against the door and, since he had now committed them to unreasonable force, Leona, Ursa, and Ellis lunged with him, pushing and shoving with all their strength. The door resisted . . . resisted . . . then yielded, swinging inward with a surrender so complete that Jackie stumbled forward and fell, sprawling on the gray carpet of a large sitting room. As Ursa, Leona, and Ellis charged in, they leaped across him as well as they could.

Christo was running for a door on the other side of the room, and before any of them had taken in the geography of the place, he had dived through it and slammed it behind him. However, there was no lock on this second door.

"Quickly!" yelled Ellis.

And then, somewhere beyond the door, a child began to cry.

"Shelley!" wailed Leona, anguish and relief mingling in her voice while Jackie and Ellis heaved, yet again, at the second door, pushing at it with their shoulders while their feet skidded on the gray carpet. Here we go again, Ellis thought, somewhere in that curious, parallel existence in which he was not a participant but a watcher witnessing his own adventures. On his left, a window looked out across the city toward the river estuary and the sea. In front of this window stood a handsome table, and on the table lay a pair of binoculars. Ellis felt sure that if he had had time to pick them up and peer into them, if he had had time to focus those binoculars, he would have found it possible to make out many details in Moncrieff Street . . . Phipps's portrait, perhaps, or the Land-of-Smiles. The door gave a little, and then a little more, cracking against something heavy that was being pushed against it.

"Christo!" yelled Ursa. "Come on! This is crazy! Christo!"

"I'm not crazy!" Christo screamed back. Ellis could tell he was some distance from the door. "Call me crazy and you'll be sorry."

There was a sliding sound that Ellis recognized, without being sure exactly what it was he was hearing . . . a drawer closing, perhaps. The remains of his hangover swept through him, but he set his teeth, leaned his whole weight against the door as implacably as he could.

"Christo?" called Ursa. "Please!"

"Push!" grunted Ellis, and the door opened a little farther. Beyond it he saw light moving across glass.

The child's cry, which had been a tired grizzling, became a shriek, then diminished as if it were vanishing into distance.

"Where's he taking her?" cried Leona.

"Heave!" yelled Jackie.

The door moved inward. Jackie leaped for the

widening space, stepping up, on, and over the heavy mahogany chest that had been pushed to block the door. Sliding after him, first Ursa, then Leona, then Ellis, they found themselves in the sort of room described in real estate language as the master bedroom, although its dusty-rose pink draperies and voluptuous cushions suggested it belonged to a mistress rather than a master. Open French windows led onto a tiny balcony, and on the balcony rail, feet in black running shoes were stretched up on tiptoe. Two legs, sheathed in black jeans, strained above the shoes, but the rest of Christo was invisible, for he was in the act of pulling himself up over one of the wide, tiled lids that had half winked at Ellis the night before. The balcony was cluttered with small things—a little table on curling, iron legs, two chairs, and a folded sun umbrella. Taking all this in as he moved forward, Ellis had an image of the Kilmers sitting there, working out a trendy separation while exhaust fumes drifted up from the street below.

As Ellis made for the balcony, Jackie dived forward, too. He clearly meant to catch Christo's feet, but Leona seized him and wheeled him around, crying out ferociously as she did so and reminding him that Christo must be holding Shelley. They could not—must not—try tugging him down. As Jackie and Leona swung around each other in a brief parody of a dance, the feet on the balcony rail flexed themselves. Christo leaped upward. One foot dangled, flapping a little, as Christo struggled to drag his knee up onto the overhang. A desperate, scrabbling sound came from above the decorative lid, the vanished foot slid back into view, and the invisible child shrieked with either fear or fury, though her cry was thin and frail compared to the rising roar of traffic accelerating below. Then the waving foot vanished, the other followed it, and Christo was gone.

"Oh, no!" wailed Leo. "No, no!"

And it was her turn to dive for the French windows.

"Don't even look!" cried Ellis, for he, too, half expected to see Shelley tumble past, falling like a bundle of rags, tossed away so that Christo could make good his escape.

And even now, in the small, separate world of his own head, he was aware how sweet Leona smelled, though he also caught, faint but distinct, something he had not previously recognized—the tang of antiseptic.

Meanwhile, Jackie, grabbing the iron post at the corner of the balcony, had leaped onto a chair, then onto the table and, in the same flow of movement, onto the balcony rail, grabbing the edge of the roof as he did so. Almost at once, Christo kicked him. Crying out in alarm, Jackie swayed backward, Ursa springing to catch him, and screaming as she did so. But Jackie, being Jackie, had already saved himself.

"He's got Shelley in a backpack," he shouted down to them. "Hey!" he cried, grasping the gutter once more and leaning backward so he could get a better view. "Chris! Don't be such a shit."

Christo's voice drifted back to them, perfectly

clear but a little eerie, as if he were shouting from another dimension.

"Leave me alone! If you follow me, I'll throw the
kid over. And don't call me Chris!"

The knot between Jackie's shoulders seemed to
loosen itself. He looked down at the others on the balcony. "Call the cops!" he said in a low voice. It was the
shape of his lips rather than the sound of the words that
gave the message. "Now! Like *now*!"

Leona, who had also squeezed onto the balcony,
turned and ran into the bedroom to look for a
phone.

"Shall I go after him?" Jackie added, still speaking
very softly and sounding more dubious than Ellis had
ever heard him sound before.

"No!" said Ellis, entirely sure of himself. "You're his
enemy. Come down!"

Jackie jumped effortlessly from the balcony rail.
"Someone ought to talk to him . . . distract him for a
bit," he said, looking shaken, as if, for the first time, he
really believed Shelley might die.

"I will," said Ursa.

"No," said Ellis. "I will. He isn't frightened of me.
He's used to beating me up. Besides," he added, "I
know what to say to him." And, instantly, things shifted
in his head, and he knew, knew for certain, that he was
the one who had a message for Christo.

"He's flipped!" said Jackie. "He's totally flipped."

They could hear Leona dialing a number in the
bedroom, and then hear her babbling rather desper-

ately as she spoke, presumably to the police. Suddenly her voice seemed to fail. Standing in the doorway like a ghost, she stared at them, holding out the phone stretched to the limit of its cord. "You tell them," she said. "I can't! I don't even know exactly where we are."

As Jackie grabbed the phone and went into the bedroom, and Ellis moved farther out onto the balcony, a voice, wailing like the parody of a ghost-voice in a horror film, came floating down from above them. "Ursie! Urrr-sie!"

"Yes! On the roof," Ellis heard Jackie saying.

"Ursie!" called the voice once more. "Hey, Ursie! *Talk* to me!"

"He's up there now," Jackie was saying in the background. "He's on a sort of platform. There's scaffolding everywhere."

"Urrr-sie!" wailed Christo. "I'm not to be trusted. Talk to me!

Ursa looked at the balcony rail and roof above. "You'll have to hold me!" she said to Ellis. "I'm not great with heights."

"Oh, shit!" cried Jackie, looking through the open doors and reading her intention. The phone clattered abruptly as he dropped the receiver, a voice quacking faintly, asking questions, then probably asking them again. "You're not to!" Jackie yelled at Ursa.

Then he was beside her, seizing her arm.

Up above them, Christo called out once more. "If you don't come and talk to me, Ursie, I'll jump! Life's a bitch, anyway. I'll jump—and take the kid with me."

"You're just not *tall* enough to get onto the roof," Jackie was telling Ursa, shaking her as he spoke. "Listen to me! *I* can't get onto that roof. *I'm* not tall enough. Neither are you. Christo could because he's a tall guy. Tall and mad!"

"Jump-ing!" yelled Christo. "Bye-bye baby!"

Leona flung her arms over her head and crouched down as if the sky were crashing onto her.

"I'll put it out of its misery!" shouted Christo, which was what he had said many years ago as he had pushed Ellis, again and again, under the water.

As Jackie and Ursa hissed and struggled, Ellis scrambled onto the table, stepped onto the balcony rail, then slowly straightened. The balcony rail pressed into the balls of his feet, which were set at such awkward angles that it proved difficult to move with any confidence. So, he stood there like a dancer, frozen in the middle of a complicated step. Below him, the street crawled with cars, probably all looking for places to park, and he began to hear voices drifting up in a smoke of sound. Holding on to the post at the corner of the balcony, he moved carefully, altering the angle of his feet. As he did so, he happened to glance down, and the fall to the street below suddenly swam into focus. It was a long way down. Ellis understood that indeed he *might* fall, but forced himself to feel a sort of amused patience with his fear. Then he straightened, swung one foot around, reached up, grabbed the gutter, and, at last, dared to look for Christo and Shelley. He did not have to look far.

"Jump-ing!" Christo was calling, almost singing. And in his ritual song he sounded free from all the things that were dragging Ellis down—free from fear, free from love, free from any kind of compassion. Christo was being playful, just as he had been playful when he had so nearly drowned Ellis, all those years ago. And, remembering, Ellis knew just why Christo felt so confident. He was doing what he was good at . . . he was being a tormentor. He was fulfilled.

A sharp slope of tiles faced Ellis, climbing at an angle until it met a vertical wall. The orange pipes of scaffolding crisscrossed it, looking as if they were trying to scribble the stone out of existence. There, poised above him, on a long, narrow platform, stood Christo, standing tall as he carelessly shrugged his way out of the backpack. Ellis glimpsed a small arm waving an apparent good-bye. The sound of a wail, much more insistent now that he and Shelley were almost face-to-face, reached his ears. Christo propped the backpack against an orange pipe that rose vertically behind him. Ellis tried to work out if there was enough space between the platform and the wall for the backpack, together with the child it held, to tumble away down the stone face of the old library.

"Jumping . . . ," Christo cried almost casually, bending his knees, straightening them again, and then bending them once more.

"Hey!" Ellis yelled back, relieved to hear his own voice sounding almost as lighthearted as Christo's own, and completely unthreatening. "It's me!"

On the platform above him, Christo stood stock-still, staring down at Ellis. He did not seem to recognize him.

"Who the fuck are you?" he cried, and then exclaimed incredulously, "Ellis?" His voice altered. "Ellis! What's *happened* to you?" He sounded distracted rather than angry. But Ellis—a kitten so easy to drown—was no danger to Christo.

"They hit on me to be the transport," said Ellis. He raised his free hand, opening it to show that there was no weapon concealed in it.

"God, look at you!" Christo said. "I didn't know you." He sounded quite reasonable. "What have they done to you?"

"I'm just the transport," Ellis repeated.

"That was *you* driving them?" said Christo. "I thought you were some no-hoper from the Land-of-Smiles."

Ellis bent his knees, crouching a little, then sprang upward as hard as he could. The gutter cut into him as, floundering and clumsy, he struggled to inch himself forward, refusing to acknowledge that he was in any danger. Indeed, clumsiness was an advantage. Christo would not allow himself to be approached by anyone clever or competent.

"No closer!" cried Christo, shaking the backpack ominously. Shelley let out a tired grizzling, almost as if she already knew crying was not worth the trouble.

"Just let me . . . ," began Ellis, making himself sound as if he were in rather more difficulty than he actually was. "Can't I just . . . "

173

Christo visibly relaxed at the sound of Ellis's bumbling anxiety. He watched him get one knee onto the edge of the roof, watched him push forward yet again, and then lie extended, panting as he sprawled on the tiles. Secretly, Ellis knew he could have used his impetus to scrabble farther up the slope, but felt sure, in an instinctive way, that a competent spidering upward might have alarmed Christo.

"I've got something to tell you," called Ellis. "A sort of message from the past. Can I come on up?"

"I'll jump," said Christo, though he sounded a little bored repeating this to Ellis. "And I'll take the kid with me."

"Yes, I know," said Ellis. "It's just that I wouldn't mind being able to sit up. I mean, you *know* me."

"What's this *message* of yours?" asked Christo, his voice becoming the languid voice of the master.

"I can't tell you from here," said Ellis in a tone that deliberately whined. "If I could just–"

"Oh, Jesus!" said Christo impatiently. "Okay . . . come on up. Just don't *try* anything."

Ellis took a deep breath and began to wriggle upward and onward. Christo watched him with apparent amusement, sinking down on his haunches, then seating himself beside the backpack. By now, Ellis had lost the advantage of his original thrust toward the platform. He had planned to act an incompetent clumsiness, but found he did not have to act. His nails scraped on the tiles, his toes arched inward, pushing as well as they could, though there was nothing much

174

to push against. He slid backward a little, flattening himself and closing his eyes as he did so. Unbidden, the image of Leona advanced toward him through a tunnel of shadow and light. Abruptly, he imagined himself dead and Leona busy with his body, giving him the start of a smile with which to face eternity. Ellis scrabbled again, and this time found purchase on the tiles. The fingers of his left hand, straining upward, hooked themselves around a section of orange scaffolding. Christo aimed a half-playful kick at him, but Ellis was prepared for that, and bent his head sideways. Christo's foot struck his shoulder, but he was holding on tightly by then. And after that, it was easy. Without looking at Christo (for he knew it was important not to look directly at Christo, in case he, himself, accidentally suggested a challenge, defiance, or even pity), he pulled himself up, then up again, until he sat panting at last on the same platform Christo was occupying, one hand possessively grasping the top bar of the backpack that leaned between them.

Shelley, distracted by Ellis's arrival, had stopped grizzling. She turned her head to stare at him. It seemed that every thread of her silver fair hair stood on end, reminding Ellis vividly of the fringe of the shawl that had been wrapped around the stolen computer. How childish, how strangely innocent that chase across the hills seemed from up here on the platform, with Christo watching him across the head of the child. A strong smell assaulted him. Shelley was stinking, and

175

he realized that Christo would not have fed or changed her all day.

But Ellis knew he must not look too interested or involved. So he sighed and glanced away, pretending that he and Christo were two mountaineers who, having reached the summit, were now entitled to rest and admire the view. He was looking down on an expanse of roofs, a geography of corrugated iron, hard angles broken by the pillowy green of trees. The hunched shoulders of distant willows marked the line of the river, and, beyond them, the mirror glass of a bank reflected blue sky and white clouds in a way that made them look more exact, yet somehow less real, than sky and clouds in a painting.

"Did your lot call the police?" asked Christo sulkily.

Ellis, looking down into the street below, saw the roof of a police car, and people beginning to collect and stare upward. Incredibly, one of them had what looked like a video camera pointed toward them. The stage on which he found himself might be a little narrow, but he had what an actor needed most: He had a crowd ready to applaud him. It occurred to him that, deep down, Christo, too, might relish an audience.

"Ursa phoned, I think," he said, as if it didn't matter too much, and found he had had practice with this sort of voice. He had used it recently, over and over again, when talking to people about Simon. For this was the voice that allowed him to acknowledge Simon's death and yet prevented others from guessing just how Simon's final expression dominated his thoughts and even his dreams. And once he had Simon's image fixed in his head, Ellis took it prisoner, focusing on it. This time, Simon's ghost would not set itself free from him. He was commanding it because he might well have a use for it. "Ursa's frightened be- cause"—he jerked his head sideways at Shelley—"be- cause of the kid."

"Yeah, well, so she should be," said Christo. "I mean, Ursie's nothing . . . *nothing!* She's not as pretty as Leona, and she runs on and on about going to the uni- versity as if it were a big deal or something. And she lives . . . well, you know where she lives, don't you?" He broke off. "I wanted her to move in with me. I could have got away from my crowd and she could have got away from hers. She was so bloody *lucky,*" he cried suddenly. "She had the chance to get away from that dump she lives in. And that dreary old shit-head, Monty."

Ellis did not know how to reply. "Nice thought of yours—I mean, trying to share your luck," he began awkwardly, but Christo was unexpectedly infuriated by this.

"Share my luck?" he cried. "What's lucky about me? You think I enjoy having parents acting so *smart* about getting separated? *'Oh, yes! We've screwed every- thing up! Let's buy some champagne and make a joke of it.'* They're so *up* themselves. And everyone behaves as if having money's such a great blessing."

"Be real! It is," said Ellis mildly. "Especially if you haven't got any," he added.

"It doesn't buy happiness," said Christo, sounding as if this were a brand-new idea. He turned his head, frowning at Ellis. "You used to go around with Simon . . . Simon . . . Simon Carroll, wasn't it? That kid who did himself in a few months ago. Well, his family was rolling. And it didn't help him. You know, my old man is just walking away. He's off to Wellington. Well, he's not unloading it all on me."

"Unloading what?" asked Ellis, without any clear idea what Christo was talking about.

"Everything," said Christo with a sort of confused discontent. "My mother! All that stuff!" His tone was one of loathing. "You ought to hear her. 'We'll really have to get to know each other now,' she keeps on saying. (Laugh! Laugh!) 'We'll have such a lot of fun.' What she means is, I'll be there to do the housework and be her chauffeur and feed the dog if she decides to stay out all night. Well, fuck it! I might just do a Simon Carroll on them."

He rattled the backpack, though this time with less conviction, Ellis thought. And he felt himself feeding on that uncertainty. He felt himself silently growing in power. "Not worth it," he said softly.

"Not worth it for a wimp like you!" declared Christo, his mouth pulled down in an aggressive sneer. And, at last, Ellis, catching Christo's restless gaze, looked deeply into his eyes and smiled. Involuntarily, Christo leaned away from him. Ellis promptly leaned forward across the backpack.

"I'll tell you why it's not worth it," he said, his voice calm, even quiet, the voice of a master. "Just shut up and listen!" he went on with soft urgency. The skull tattoo suddenly stung under his sleeve. He thought he could actually feel it smiling sympathetically as he smiled himself. "Because it might prove that you're the wimp, and a bit of a voyeur, too!" he added triumphantly. He saw he had confused Christo. "I mean," he went on, desperate to work on what felt like an advantage, "I've had thoughts like that . . . that dying is the great, exciting, ultimate act, beyond anything else that anyone can do, and that everyone would be sorry when I was gone, and so on. The thing is, sitting up here, you're thinking—you can't help thinking—that you'll be around to lap up other people's misery. . . . I mean, you're imagining your dad suffering and being sorry at last, and your mom crying over her dear little boy. And you think they'll suddenly realize how precious you were, and that you'll have the fun of hearing them moan about how much they loved you, and how much they wish they'd been nicer to you, and how terrible it's been for them to lose you. And so on! But you *won't* hear anyone crying for you, and you *won't* see anyone being sorry, because you won't be there at all! You won't be anywhere, and you won't be anything, and even the people who love you will begin to forget you almost at once. People don't mean to forget—they just can't help it. You'll just start fading."

And now Ellis felt himself filled with the power of true knowledge. Though he had missed the chance to say these things to Simon, his persistent but fading friend, strangely enough, he now had the chance to explain what he understood to Christo, whom he had always hated. Bits and pieces rushed together, drawn from the present and the past, to fit into a single, unswerving form. Voices that had never had anything to say to one another in real life ran together inside him so that Leona's words sang through Simon's. He must use everything he knew, showing no secret awe, no hidden respect for Simon's choice.

"Big deal!" Christo was saying. "I don't want to *be* anything. That's the point—"

"Listen!" said Ellis, daring to interrupt him now. "Simon drank half a bottle of whisky, then poisoned himself . . . and all I can think is what a stupid, fucking idiot he was."

He was surprised, not by the sadness in his voice, but by his own savage scorn. It sounded utterly genuine. (And it is! he thought almost simultaneously. Suddenly, out of the blue, this is exactly what I think of Simon choosing to die. I'm sad, but . . . what a fool he was.) "He dreamed about making people sorry," Ellis went on. "And they *were* sorry. But he didn't *enjoy* any of it in the way he thought he would. Because he was nowhere. All anyone could do for him was push the fluid out of his body—that's called purging—and fill him with embalming fluid so he wouldn't stink too soon. Of course, they closed his eyes, they tidied him up—they can use cosmetics with lead in them on dead people. Did you know that?" He looked at Christo critically. "Might improve you a bit. And someone . . . someone gave him a nice expression, but all that was for his mom and dad."

"Shut up!" protested Christo. "Anyhow, you don't know if he could see himself or not," he added in a sulky voice. Ellis could feel, almost as if it were happening to him personally, that energy and excitement were draining out of Christo, just as the summer daylight was beginning to drain out of the sky above the city.

"He was *dead,*" said Ellis, nodding his head slowly and deliberately. "If there is a life after death, it wasn't what Simon imagined it would be. It can't be imagined. All we can truly understand is real life, and in real life, Simon was a fool . . . a dead fool."

"You haven't the least idea, have you?" Christo suddenly screamed at him. Though his voice had regained its desperation, it had lost all its earlier confidence. He grabbed at the chrome bar at the top of the backpack, tilting it down over the sloping tiles so that Shelley must have stared down into the balcony where Jackie, Ursa, and Leona were clustered, staring up, mouths open. Leona hid her face against Ursa, and Ursa, Ellis saw, took a breath and put her hand out to Jackie. But Ellis put out his own right hand and grabbed the nearest part of the backpack frame himself, which Christo had, in a way, given him the chance to do. As if he were now somehow set free from any responsibility, Christo promptly gave the backpack a push—a rather indecisive push that would have been enough, however, to topple

Shelley into the void had Ellis not been holding the frame so tightly. The backpack made a half spin on the rounded, lower corner of its frame. The corner pivoted on the platform, and then slipped inward. Shelley stared down into the abyss but remained silent.

The backpack was surprisingly heavy. It jerked on Ellis's arm. It dragged at his shoulder. As he was tilted forward he felt some sinew in his neck tightening like a guitar string, but he did not let go. Instead, he flung his free arm around one of the orange pipes that rose behind the platform and, struggling, he once more straightened the backpack, little by little. Then, feeling in control at last, he turned and smiled at Christo.

"You going to pull *me* back?" asked Christo threateningly, staring at Ellis as if he had been transformed into a supernatural stranger.

"Save yourself," said Ellis. Then he added, "Corpses fart sometimes. Did you know that?" He had only known it himself for about three hours. Christo, who had been bending his knees a little, quickly straightened them. "You could donate your organs to someone who really needs them," Ellis added. "It could be the best thing you ever did."

They continued to stare at each other, up there on the platform above Foley Street. Then Ellis spoke again.

He did not use the voice he had used in the Shakespeare scene that had marked the end of his school life, or the sort of dramatic horror that had won him such applause, but a *puzzled* voice–the voice of someone working out their true thoughts and coming to a dreadful conclusion.

> *"Ay, but to die, and go we know not where,*
> *To lie in cold obstruction and to* rot–"

"Poetry?" yelled Christo, trying to break the spell that was settling over him.

"No, no–just listen! Listen," said Ellis. He was not talking so very loudly, but his urgency, the sibilance of the "s" in "listen," somehow accumulated authority– certainly more authority than his companion was able to command with all his shouting. "Just listen!" repeated Ellis. "You need to know. *You* need to know more than anyone.

> *"To lie in cold obstruction and to* rot; . . ."

The word "rot" emerged like a bullet, shot from the trigger of his tongue.

> *"This sensible warm motion to become*
> *A kneaded clod; . . ."*

Ellis, with one arm crooked around the scaffolding and one hand grasping the backpack, jiggled a little, emphasizing the words, and allowed his feet to dance in the air below the platform, which shook to the rhythm of his movement.

"Hey!" cried Christo in alarm, grasping the nearest

orange pipe himself and clinging to it as if the dance were more dangerous for him than it was for Ellis.

"and the delighted spirit, . . ."

Ellis continued,

> *"To bathe in fiery floods, or to reside*
> *In thrilling regions of the thick-ribbed ice,*
> *To be imprisoned in the viewless winds*
> *And blown with restless violence round about*
> *The pendent world; or to be worse than worst,"*

cried Ellis, puzzling it out for Simon as well as for himself.

> *"Of those that lawless and incertain thoughts*
> *Imagine howling!—'tis too horrible!*
> *The weariest and most loathed worldly life*
> *That age, ache, penury and imprisonment*
> *Can lay on nature is a paradise*
> *To what we fear of death."*

The puzzling voice changed as he spoke the last lines. Ellis spat out the final word, grimacing a little at Christo, who now cowered before him. Yet Ellis was speaking in a state that, later, he was to describe to himself as exaltation. For the first time, he thought, he had the words completely right. The weight fell from his shoulders, the tension vanished from around his throat. In the back of his mind, Simon smiled faintly.

Christo's stillness altered. His nose wrinkled as if

he might be about to cry, but the sound that came out of his open mouth was the sort of laugh that might have been laughed by a windup doll. "Are you trying to counsel me with *Shakespeare*?"

("Timing's everything," said the director's voice, speaking out of Ellis's memory.)

Then, somewhere out on Foley Street, he heard a clock chime . . . the same clock he had heard round about this time the night before, just before meeting Jackie. The clock struck the quarter hour with a soft but significant chime. "Now!" that final fading stroke declaimed. Twenty-four hours, thought Ellis in amazement. It was saying "Once upon a time" last night, and now it's telling us to live happily ever after. He released Christo from his stare and glanced down at Shelley.

"She's asleep," he exclaimed. "Doesn't say much for my acting."

His voice suddenly trembled. It was as if the clock had chimed the end of a magic day, and ordinary life was moving in on him once more. Christo relaxed and became more ordinary, as well.

"I don't know!" he said in the voice of a weary man. "There's no *point* in anything. Home's coming to pieces. And there's nothing I want to *do*. My father says I'm thick. He says it over and over again. And Ursa *thinks* I'm thick. I know she does."

"You probably are," said Ellis. "Me, too! But at least we're both brighter and better off than poor, bloody Simon. Let's go down."

He drew his legs up, knelt, and began, very cautiously, to slide the backpack down the sloping tiles toward the eager hands below, expecting the child to wake at any moment. But Shelley's head simply bobbled to one side, and she slept on.

"Gawd! Be careful," yelled Jackie, scrambling onto the table and stretching up toward him. "Slowly! Slowly! Don't blow it now!"

"Don't you dare fall backward," said Ursa, but she was talking to Jackie, not Ellis.

Ellis guided the backpack safely into Jackie's extended hands, and Jackie edged it down, obviously finding it heavier than he had anticipated.

"Hang on!" cried Jackie, and then, taking a breath, he slid the backpack over the gutter into the other arms stretched out to receive it.

Ellis straightened. "Hey," he called a little facetiously. "Make us a cup of tea, will you?"

"There's beer in the fridge," mumbled Christo. Ellis saw that in taking over Christo's drama, he had also stolen Christo's energy.

And he found that he had dissolved not his sadness over Simon's death, but its oppression—its power. He was free, and this freedom, coupled with exhaustion, made him feel so light, he half believed he could fly. He could leap from the building's slate eyelid and swoop down mockingly over the police car below. Careful, he told himself, and turned to Christo.

"You go down next!" he said, and saw, with a mixture of surprise and exaltation, that Christo was going to do exactly as he was told. Obediently turning, he lowered himself over the platform and slid down, first into Jackie's arms, then into the double embrace of Leona and Ursa. They could not, however, contain his final, tumbling descent. Nor did Christo try in any way to arrest his own fall. He fell heavily onto the balcony, and though he was not stunned, he lay where he fell, deliberately closing his eyes. They called his name, but he refused to look at any of them. Ellis followed. It was harder to slide down than it had been to climb up. He felt himself lose control as he inched downward, felt Jackie seize him, and wobble dangerously as he did so. They tumbled together on top of Christo.

Suddenly there were people milling around them. Names were being asked for. Someone in uniform was bending over Christo, who lay, hugging himself, knees drawn up, his eyes resolutely closed. Then it was Ellis's turn.

"You were so marvelous," Leona was crying, and she flung her arms around Ellis and kissed him, just as the heroine kisses the hero at the end of the story . . . but not quite. Ellis, hugging her back, took a breath and smelled that faint scent, in which once again he thought he could distinguish the sting of antiseptic. But this time he laughed. After all, he really was the hero, not just the boy being kissed by the beautiful girl, or the person who had saved the child, but the actor who had triumphed on the narrow stage.

AFTER

The next day, Ellis found himself returning to the Land-of-Smiles to collect his house key and driver's license, carelessly left behind in room Number Nine. He biked across the city on a bicycle that he had not used since passing his driving test. Once at the Land-of-Smiles, he propped the bike against a fence and carefully locked it with a new chain and padlock. He looked at the rust and graffiti, then saluted the image of Phipps peering at him from the white wall on the far side of Kurl-Up & Dye. The last time, he was thinking. I won't be coming here again. Yet, as he walked toward the motel door, he found that he was being welcomed. Harley, jogging by, waved at him. Then Prince appeared around the corner of the house. He did not pause but strode toward Ellis, holding his right hand high.

"Give me five, man!" he said, words which Ellis thought belonged exclusively to American sitcoms.

Hastily, he raised his own hand to slap Prince's as they passed each other. "Yo, bro!" said Prince, walking on. However, it was the door of the Land-of-Smiles itself that welcomed him in, outlined, even in broad daylight, by the streaming electric arrows that rose, perpetually, on the right, arching above the door, and diving into nothing on the left. He went through the lobby, through the dining room and made confidently for the kitchen.

Ellis had only known this kitchen for a single day, but now it seemed as familiar as the kitchen in his own house. All the same, it was still capable of springing a surprise. Since yesterday, someone had set a Christmas tree in the corner. Though the dark branches were as yet undecorated, glittering worms of tinsel were tangled together beneath it, escaping from battered boxes that had obviously seen many other Christmases.

Ursa was sitting at the table on her own, pages spread around her. She looked up suspiciously, then, seeing who it was, beamed at Ellis.

"Hi!" she said. "Our hero! Our total, utter hero! Star of scaffolding and television! Grab a coffee."

Ellis, who had certainly not been planning to stay for coffee, found himself turning, like a Land-of-Smiles habitué, toward the coffee machine, and tugging one of the waxed cardboard cups out of the holder.

"You looked great on television," Ursa said to his back. "Just right! Brave . . . modest . . . sweetly shy! Tired but gallant. Pity you didn't have your curls, but not to worry. Might have been overdoing it!"

"Yesterday," said Ellis, "I was walking along planning the next year or two. Then I met Jackie, and in the following twenty-four hours, I did every single thing I'd been planning to do over the coming year. I mean, it was my first day home from school." He looked at Ursa to see how she received this revelation. Ursa's expression did not change. "And I got drunk," said Ellis. "And shot around in a car chase, and ended up on a sort of stage high above the city. I–I sort of fell in love. . . ." Once again he glanced a little defiantly at her but, once again, she did not look as if she were likely to laugh at him. "And I brought back my mother's car, smelling of stale piss, and with the back-door handle missing *and* a scrape along one side. *And* I was suddenly bald. *And* I've been tattooed, though I haven't told my mum about that yet. Mum and Dad were furious with me when I finally did get home–I mean, not just grumpy, but *really* furious. But, suddenly, there I was on TV with people praising me! My father forgave me, and my mother stopped complaining. After all, the car *is* insured. It's gone to the repair shop to be assessed, so I had to ride over here on a bike. Bit of a comedown!"

"Monty's getting *his* car back today," said Ursa. "We won't need yours again for a while. Have you just called in for the fun of it?"

"I left some stuff in Number Nine," said Ellis, pointing toward the door. "I'll just go and get it."

"I'll come with you," said Ursa. "The door's locked." She walked over to the coffee machine and shifted it a little. Ellis saw with surprise that there was a small cupboard set in the wall behind it.

"Leona said something about frightening you," Ursa went on, opening the cupboard and taking out a bunch of keys. "My guess is she suddenly mentioned her work. It disconcerts a lot of people when they find out."

Ellis stared defiantly at the back of her head while she concealed the little door with the coffee machine once more.

"It doesn't matter," he said.

"Did you throw up?" she asked, turning and smiling. "Some people do. Well, metaphorically they do."

"I think I did—metaphorically, that is," sighed Ellis.

"It's a private test of hers," said Ursa, flinging wide the door to the line of rooms and looking out toward the rubbish bags with calm pleasure, rather as if she were surveying a well-kept lawn and rose garden. Ellis saw that she was wearing a ring on the third finger of her left hand—small, bright, and ostentatiously false—a pearl held by shiny, gold claws.

"A test? Well, I failed it," said Ellis. Clutching his cup of coffee, he meekly followed Ursa to the door of Number Nine.

"Did she mention our own particular, family soap opera?" Ursa asked, unlocking the door and pushing it open with her bare foot.

"No," Ellis said, and hesitated. "But Phipps did."

Putting his cup down on the chest of drawers beside the bed, he jiggled open the top drawer. There was his house key. There was his driver's license. He was being reunited with the bits and pieces that made him a man of the world.

"Phipps loves the story," said Ursa. "It's almost like yesterday's gossip to him. Of course, we've been neighbors for a long time."

Ellis tucked his key and driver's license into a top pocket, picked up his coffee, and followed Ursa out of the room. After she had locked the door once more, he trailed after her to the kitchen.

"How's the coffee?" she asked.

Ellis looked into the cardboard cup with the intensity of Fox gazing into her glowing crystal. It was certainly black. He already knew it was probably a little burnt.

"You don't have to drink it," Ursa said, sitting down beside her papers and books once more.

"I've actually grown to like it this way," Ellis said, interested to find that this was almost true. How could one come to feel *nostalgic* about something like burned coffee within twenty-four hours? "It still tastes like coffee—just coffee on another planet."

Ursa nodded.

"If you live our sort of life you get to love things that don't turn out quite right," she said. "You begin to enjoy the . . . the *faultiness* of the world because it ties you into your real life."

"Hang on!" said Ellis. "Are you saying that being faulty is *truer* than not being faulty."

"It's second nature for me to think so by now," said

Ursa. "Something goes wrong! 'Hey! *There* you are,' I exclaim, as if I've met a dear old friend down at the shops. My dad was–" She broke off. "Oh," she said at last, smiling the sort of smile that lifts one corner of the mouth and twists the other down, "he could be lovely . . . he *was* lovely, played games, joked, cuddled us, and rubbed us with his bristly chin before he shaved. Mind you, he did lose his temper from time to time. Mum called it 'getting his Irish up', though Dad wasn't Irish in any way. We took it for granted for years, though I think Leo and I were beginning to understand there was something a bit excessive–a bit odd . . ." She paused, then began again briskly. "One night, Dad woke us all up–Leona, me, Wolf and Felix–"

"Wolf and Felix?" Ellis said uncertainly.

"My brothers," said Ursa. "There were five of us back then. 'We're going to look at the stars,' my father said. 'I've got a telescope, and it's a lovely night.' He made Leo carry Fox, while he carried the telescope–it could easily have been a telescope–wrapped in a bit of sacking.

"So off we all went toward our back door. Mind you, I don't think any of us *really* thought we were going to look at the stars . . . well, Felix might have, and Fox was only a baby. But Leo, Wolf, and I knew that something else was going on. Hard to tell now, because you know how memories keep on shifting and changing. Anyhow, as we crossed the sitting room to the front door, I looked across into the kitchen. The door was partly open and I could make out bare legs, and the edge of my mother's dressing gown, and her feet, one with a slipper on and the other bare. My father saw me notice, but he just smiled. 'It's a game, sweetheart . . . don't worry, it's just a game,' he said.

"So we went over the road to the cemetery—in at the gate we used today. And we stopped close to Rose Phipps—she was our Phippo's great-grandmother, may she rest in pieces! We stood there in the night. It wasn't dark. It never is, is it, in the center of the city? That's why we couldn't really have looked at the stars.

"'Life is too terrible to be lived,' my father said, out there among the tombstones. Of course, it wasn't a telescope he had in that sackcloth. It was a gun. Leo says she knew right then what he was going to do, even though she couldn't actually see the gun. She screamed at him and tried to hide Fox. But, before her scream was properly over, my father had shot Wolf and then Felix. . . ." Ursa scratched her head, looking at Ellis and making a rueful face. "Leo was hugging Fox like she hugged Shelley last night, sort of arching over her, doing everything she could to hide her. And Dad stood looking down at us, as if we were the ones who had done it all. We were yelling our heads off by then, and Dad was saying, 'Shh! Shh! Shh!' louder and louder—like an old steam train shunting. Then, suddenly, he—he just put the barrel of the gun in his own mouth and pulled the trigger."

Ursa stopped talking. They stared at each other.

"Look," said Ellis rather desperately. "I don't know what to say to all that. It's—well, it's too much, isn't it—

too much of *something* to reply to. If you're trying to show me that things have been worse for you than they have for me . . . that I'm a lucky, rich, spoiled kid . . ."

"No!" exclaimed Ursa. "Nothing like that. Mostly, I don't tell this story because it's all old stuff, though it's part of us forever. But I'm telling you as a sort of, well, a sort of funny Christmas present. I'm giving you a bit of our lives because you saved Shelley. And Shelley saved, balances things out–just a little bit. And I also wanted to explain something about us, because for ages we've lived . . . eye to eye with death, and it's not all that bad. From some angles, at least, there's a bit of a lazy smile in those empty old eye sockets. Sorry if I'm sounding a bit morbid, because I don't think we are morbid, any of us. But we've had to make ourselves companionable with death. Leo, in particular, gets impatient with people shuddering. Me–well, I don't blame the people who do shudder. After all, we're engineered to live on and on, if we possibly can, and shuddering proves the engine is in good working order. It's natural to die and it's natural to fear dying, so it was really good that you managed to make Christo shudder last night . . . you and Shakespeare, that is."

"What happened to you afterward?" asked Ellis, ignoring these comments.

Ursa threw up her hands.

"Oh, everything!" she said. "We lived with an aunt for a while, but there was trouble, trouble, trouble . . . and social welfare stepped in to find us a foster home.

195

Well, we wound up with Monty during his grand days. He was quite the guru of foster care back then . . . thrilled with the Orono Indians, thrilled with his own ideas, and thrilling a lot of other people with them, too. And we Hammonds had a happy time with Monty and his wife, May . . . they really came to love us. And we loved them. Then Monty had his great, devastating, mucky, middle-aged love affair."

The title of a book he had never read came into Ellis's head. "Was it something like *Lolita*?" he asked.

Ursa shrugged her shoulders. "Everyone mentions *Lolita*," she said. "It might have been a bit like that. Anyhow, Monty not only wrecked his career, but he wrecked himself . . . everything. There was a court case, and we were divided between two foster homes for a while, Leo and me in one, Fox in another. We had to fight our way back together, and then fight to get back to Monty and May. Leo and I were determined, and we did get back with them at last, but it wasn't the same. I mean, May had forgiven Monty—but then she died. And he copped out in quite a big way . . . said he wanted to 'embrace the gutter'. So he bought the dear old Land-of-Smiles, and we've stayed here ever since because we've wanted to stay with him. He needs looking after. And we like it here. End of story."

"Don't you ever think of shifting?" Ellis asked. But Ursa did not seem to hear him.

"About the time Leona was looking for a first job, we went to a funeral. Leo met David Dommett and heard there was a job going at Dommett & Christie. It's suited her well, because she needs to be with people to whom death is . . . just a part of things. Well, mysterious, maybe, but ordinary, too. No exaggerated reverence, either, because that's often disguised horror."

"No shuddering!" said Ellis.

"Perish the thought," agreed Ursa.

The door to the dining room opened, and Jackie waltzed into the room. He started back dramatically at the sight of Ellis. "Oh, wow!" he cried. "The Tarzan of Foley Street."

Ellis glanced over his shoulder at Ursa.

"Does *he* shudder?"

Ursa laughed. "Him?" she said. "He's in a fairyland of his own. Did you ever hear the story of the boy who set off to learn what shuddering meant? That boy was Jackie, and he's never learned." Her derisive expression changed. "Well, he just might have, listening to you last night. Do you know what he said this morning? He said he might train for a job. I nearly fell over."

"Go on! Show him the ring," said Jackie. "That's evidence of a changed life."

Ursa held out her hand with the patently false-pearl ring. It glowed rather grandly.

"It was in with the old Christmas decorations," said Jackie. "It came out of a cracker last year. Like it?"

"Very sincere!" said Ellis.

"I'd have given her a real one," Jackie went on, "but I'm opposed to the exploitation of oysters. They go to all that trouble improving bits of grit. I think they should be allowed to keep the pearls."

"I'll always wear this one," she promised him. "It's more sincere than most."

They made Ellis promise to stop in over Christmas. He laughed, finally agreed, and waved good-bye. Christmas, he thought, could only be an anticlimax to someone who had lived a whole life of love, adventure, and little dances with death—and all within twenty-four hours.

As he left the Land-of-Smiles someone said his name in a low, insistent voice. He turned. Fox rose from behind the reception counter like a column of smoke, veiled in her drifting, black shawls and holding her crystal before her.

"You are leaving!" she intoned. "You are leaving the Land-of-Smiles."

"Forever," agreed Ellis, not because he really believed it, but because the occasion seemed to demand a dramatic statement.

"Nah!" said Fox in her natural voice, then reverted, almost at once to her more portentous one. "Nay! You have become one of us. You will return. I see you dancing here when Ursa marries Jackie."

She slid from behind the small counter, and followed him as he strolled toward his bike.

"When Ursa marries Jackie? You might just as well say 'Forever'," said Ellis, grinning down at her, and thinking of the Christmas-cracker ring. "It's more sincere than most," Ursa had said, and Ellis felt sure she had meant it.

"Anyhow, you'll be back *before* then," said Fox sternly. "You won't be able to stay away. Not because of Leo, either. She's going to marry David Dommett, and you'll dance at her wedding, too." She peered into the glass. Then she looked up.

"You're going to marry me," she announced. "But not for ages yet," she added comfortingly.

"Oh, sure!" said Ellis, smiling again, unchaining his bike and pulling it away from the fence.

"You're seventeen now," Fox said. "And you think there's nothing left to look forward to. But you'll be twenty-seven in ten years . . . and I'll be twenty-one. Look forward to me! You'll think I'm just amazing by then. I will be, too."

She gave him a clear, confident smile. Her teeth were very white.

"How do you know I'm seventeen?" asked Ellis, lifting the front wheel of his bike out of the long grass and turning it toward Garden Lane. He paused, frowning. "How do you know that I think there's nothing left to look forward to?"

"The glass tells all!" she cried triumphantly, elevating her crystal. The sunlight struck through the glass and it seemed to give off crimson rays. "The glass tells all," she repeated.

"Yeah, sure!" said Ellis. "Oh, well! Roll on, Christmas!"

"See you!" she said, waving the red glass at him as he climbed onto his bicycle.

"See you!" Ellis replied, waving, and wobbling just a little.

"Not yet!" she called, running beside his bike as he pedalled toward the gateway. "You don't see me yet! But you will! You'll see me in my true wonder."

Ellis waved again, pedalling more confidently as he got going, a man sorting though a whole lifetime's experience as he set out once more into the dangerous world.

"Ellis in Wonderland," Fox shouted after him, dancing, and laughing raucously. "Ellis in Wonderland!"

Echoes leaped back from rusting corrugated iron, subsiding walls, perhaps even from the painted Phipps spying on them from between the buildings. Ellis rode off down Garden Lane, the sound of Fox's laughter following him all the way.